# GROWING UP MALE

## The Psychology of Masculinity

### B. Mark Schoenberg

**Bergin & Garvey**
**Westport, Connecticut • London**

**Library of Congress Cataloging-in-Publication Data**

Schoenberg, B. Mark.
    Growing up male : the psychology of masculinity / B. Mark
Schoenberg.
        p.    cm.
    Includes bibliographical references and index.
    ISBN 0-89789-344-1 (alk. paper)
    1. Masculinity (Psychology)   2. Men—Psychology.       I. Title.
BF692.5.S36   1993
155.3'32—dc20          93-18137

British Library Cataloguing in Publication Data is available.

Library of Congress Catalog Card Number: 93-18137
ISBN: 0-89789-344-1

First published in 1993

Bergin & Garvey, 88 Post Road West, Westport, CT 06881
An imprint of Greenwood Publishing Group, Inc.

Printed in the United States of America

∞™

The paper used in this book complies with the
Permanent Paper Standard issued by the National
Information Standards Organization (Z39.48-1984).

10 9 8 7 6 5 4 3 2 1

**Copyright Acknowledgment**

The author and publisher gratefully acknowledge permission to
reprint material from the following copyrighted source.

Excerpts reprinted by permission of Greenwood Publishing
Group, Inc., Westport, CT, from *Interactive Counseling*, by
B. Mark Schoenberg and Charles F. Preston. Copyright © 1983
by B. Mark Schoenberg and Charles F. Preston.

# Contents

# Preface

In Chapter 1, on the very first page of text, I make the point that "not many years ago a book dealing with the male persona would have been considered inane, somewhat beside the point." Men had no persona, they played no role: they were men, and that was the long and the short of it. That was the traditional, the patriarchal, and of course the biblical perspective. Men were good at problem-solving, at decision-making. It taxes the imagination to believe that anyone could believe that men were free from problems, but the first precept of conventional wisdom held that men had to keep certain things to themselves. This was the expectation; indeed, it was the manly thing to do.

But times have changed, and society has grown more complex. In the process, the perception of who man is and what he stands for has changed as well. And although it is unlikely that the average man was ever as stoic as Western society wanted him to be, the stature and presence that simpler times conferred on this "traditional man" enabled him to serve as an authentic role model for young men of his acquaintance. Strong role models have not disappeared off the face of the earth, but for many youths they may be a lot harder to find.

We are in the midst of a difficult-to-categorize revolution. It is a social revolution, but it is also highly political. For the most part it has been a sexual revolution, fought more or less along the lines of gender. Someone was asked to define "ignorance and apathy"; the reply, "I don't know and I don't care," is likely the same answer most men would give to the question "How have you been affected by the [fill in the blank] revolution?" From any perspective, men have been far too complacent.

Males of all ages will find this book of interest. The younger man can consider it a roadmap, a wealth of insight into the road he must travel. The book will enable the older male to revisit his personal history, probably making better sense of it in the process. Parents of children who are "growing up male" will discover they may be able to keep a pace or two ahead of their offspring. Teachers, in secondary schools in particular, can recommend the book as resource material for students who are confronted with issues of self-worth and self-esteem.

I would like to thank Mike Doyle for his help in the original library research, and gratefully acknowledge the cooperation of Bobbi Dwyer, Susan O'Brien and Sherry O'Brien in the final preparation of the manuscript.

# Growing up Male

# 1

# Overview: Review of the Issues

The autonomous male, the independent strong achiever who can be counted
on to be always in control, is still essentially the preferred male image.
—Herb Goldberg,
*The Hazards of Being Male*

The Vice-President of the United States talks about family values and is
immediately pounced on by media critics and stand-up comedians alike.
The media has a field-day ridiculing the Vice-President, the humor of the
comedian becomes social commentary even for those who should know
better, and the significance of family values takes another plunge. So goes
the trend.

It has become trendy as well to devalue the male, his maleness, and by
extension his masculinity. The degree to which any man has been personally affected by this attitude depends on a number of factors; some are
troubled by it, many are not. Others refer to the trend and pronounce the
male to be in crisis, but that probably overstates the case.

Not many years ago a book dealing with the male persona would have
been considered inane, somewhat beside the point. Men were strong, in
control of themselves as well as their personal space. The individual man
was responsible for his personal welfare and the welfare of those
immediately at hand. This might mean different things for different
people: a peasant or working man bore responsibility for his family, a king
or emperor the welfare of all of the people of his nation-state. A regent

might be set into place to handle the responsibilities of a king who could not rule; a strong woman might assume the dominant role in a family when the man was unable or incapable of doing so. Situations such as these were camouflaged: the regent ruled at the pleasure of the king, the woman out of necessity. This patriarchal view was subscribed to by theorists and lay people alike, with the result that men were expected to cope, period. Fortunately, contemporary society empowers men to build a new and better reality for themselves. In large measure this development is a result of the success other groups in society have had in exposing basic conflicts between societal expectation and personal aspiration. These groups have gained a wide and generally receptive audience in recent decades, and no group has been more active in pursuing human rights than the women's movement. But men's issues are frequently not the same as women's, and in fact can be significantly different. Beginning with a societal evolution filtered by hundreds of cultures and continuing through innumerable physiological, emotional, social, and psychological experiences, men and women have been historically set apart. Also historically, the individual man as well as the collective cohort was directed by circumstances into the leadership or dominant role in male–female interactions. Given this historical reality, it is a bit much to argue that patriarchy, which leads to male dominance, is the result of a conspiracy.

It is historical error to argue that gender inequality somehow started with the writings of Sigmund Freud. The father of psychoanalysis wrote about the place of men and women within society, but these observations were made almost a century ago and in a different society. Feminists generally have little regard for Freud, for the most part because he seemed to believe that gender itself was a determining factor in behavioral disorders. Indeed, in one place he described hysterical phenomena as a female disorder, to be found in "saints and nuns, continent women and well-brought-up children" (Breuer and Freud, 1961, p. 11). Still, the man must not be removed from his context. In point of fact, Freud was frequently at odds with the established medical fraternity because of his liberal views. So clearly, gender discrimination did not originate with Freud. In fact, man's experience throughout the ages has worked to validate the notion of a society dominated by the male. Unequal patterns of male and female development did not result from any rational determination. The unequal patterns were brought about by elements of historical necessity that over time became patterned into a rigid belief system. Man's earliest ancestors lived in a harsh and hostile environment that placed a high premium on physical strength. The strong survived, and the weak lived exceedingly brief lives. It is no accident that the earliest works of art generally portray the male as either a valiant hunter or as a victorious combatant: art reflects reality, and hunting and fighting were principal activities for the male.

Because he was the fighter and because he was the provider, it was inevitable that the male came to be responsible for woman's welfare. This is the historical reality. Gender differentiation evolved out of actual physical, perhaps physiological, necessity. Later, the generalized belief system that grew out of the biblical stories of Adam and Eve brought additional insight to the historical evidence of gender discrimination. Add to this that the passing of time, even when expressed in hundreds of years, brought about little change in the relationship between the sexes, and one is forced to conclude that gender differences arose out of, and were perpetuated by, the requirements of the larger society. These differences became codified over a very long period of time into a system that set forth gender expectations.

The code was comprehensive: in the case of the male it was restrictive as well as prescriptive. Men were expected to be in control at all times, of themselves as well as their situation. For the individual male, winning the day often became more important than living it: a cherished folk belief held that it was better to have played the game and lost than never to have played at all. The expression was whimsical, the reality was not. The winner was lauded, perhaps idolized, but winning on any level required a modest disclaimer from the victor. In return for the acclaim, the winner was required to display his humility by minimizing the extent of his victory in the first instance, and in the second making appropriate comments about the competitive spirit displayed by his opponent. If he did not, he was thought to be ungentlemanly and certainly not worthy of the victory. There was also a code for the loser. Prior to his retreat from the field, the loser was expected to publicly congratulate the man who had bested him. A stiff upper lip was expected to mask any pain or resentment, because regardless of consequence the loser was expected to accept his loss gracefully, cheerfully, and totally without rancor. Otherwise he was referred to as a poor loser and was judged to be a man unable to play according to the rules.

Gradually, and over a very long period, factors as diverse as custom and cherished belief impacted on the reality of everyday life to produce a blueprint for male behavior. In the process, words like "manliness" and "masculinity" began to take on particularized characteristics. The word "manly" and its derivative, "manliness," came to be associated with all the virtues spelled out in the code of the winner. The words "masculine" and "masculinity" described the broader, more generic condition. To be masculine was to be male: being male could be good or it could be bad, for generally it was labeled as one or the other. "Masculine" and "male" came to be used to describe the behavior of the poor loser and the graceful winner. Equally important, words such as these took on a sexual significance that tended to mirror the word's general meaning. "Manliness" described behavior that was chivalrous, perhaps tender and sensitive. "Masculinity," on the other hand, being shorthand for gender, could be used as easily for condemnation as for praise.

Masculine imprinting begins at birth and continues into childhood, adolescence, and adulthood. Each of these periods provides a kind of laboratory in which the child growing into manhood learns to try out those attitudes and those behaviors that in time will be the pattern for his masculine self. In each developmental state the individual has to learn, as well as to process. A complication is that one can learn without understanding the process, and conversely one can experience the process and not learn. Learning and experiences impact on attitudes and behavior, conditionings become reinforced or not as the case may be. Influences are good or they are bad, a quality distinction frequently lost on the person whose destiny is being shaped. Maturing into adulthood is not an easy task for either boy or girl, man or woman. Having said that, we might also argue that the developmental tasks faced by the boy/man are the more formidable because the rules are more rigid.

## THE DOUBLE STANDARD

Bits and pieces remain, but by and large the worst abuses of the double standard are no more. Neither men nor women should grieve for the good old days "when men were men and women were women" because in fact the code made individuals of both gender victims of the system. There is a problem when attention focuses on a standard that condemned women to a life of household drudgery, generally ignoring that the same system locked men into beasts-of-burden bondage. The problem persists when attention focuses on concerns of the working woman, ignoring those of the working man. On the whole, women have gained; on the whole, men have not. In point of fact, one can argue that the gains made by women are balanced by the losses suffered by men. One can sympathize with the working woman who worries about the welfare of her children while she is at work, but this sympathy should also extend to the man who also worries about the welfare of his children while his wife is at work. It is strange that men's rights are never considered to be on the same level as those of women. Perhaps the logic can be explained as catch-up time, but an inescapable conclusion is that the female gender has gained its rights at the male's expense. Perhaps some of this was necessary, but the pendulum has swung too far in the opposite direction. It is not at all certain that men generally are cognizant of how this wide swing has affected them.

The most serious risk is that the individual will not be able to interpret the mixed signals on maleness and masculinity that the larger society is sending him. Gordon and Meth (1990) comment on the electronic media, "when men are not portrayed as tough, macho heroes, they are more likely to be wimpy buffoons than men who are expressive in a way that reflects depth of character" (p. 61). How does one behave like a man if the definition is unclear? How does a man wear his maleness? Or act out his masculinity? Uncertainties such as these weaken the bonds of fraternalism that have historically governed the way men relate to one another, which in turn will complicate the transmission of traditional masculine values. The young adult male who is not presented with a healthy concept of personality cannot build his own construct, either of self or of role. The risk will be higher in those homes where the father is either absent or ineffective. It has been a quarter-century since Lynn (1964) observed that males tend to have greater difficulty in achieving same-sex identification than females. In this context, it seems logical to assume that if boys experienced difficulty in achieving same-sex identification at a time when masculine values were respected and were firmly in place, they will encounter even greater difficulties in a time when the concept of masculinity appears to be in the process of being devalued. Traditional concepts of maleness and masculinity provided men with a set of behavioral guidelines as well as an explicit code of ethics that formed a foundation for personal construct development. A worrisome complication is that the traditional family is rapidly becoming an anachronism, and nowhere is this breakdown more evident than in family structures in the urban underclass. The nuclear and extended families formerly provided role models in addition to opportunities for same-sex identification for younger members.

It has become an article of faith for social activists that excesses brought on by the double standard could not be addressed as long as the ideals of manliness or masculinity were in place. Moreover, the notion that any recognition of gender difference would serve to perpetuate role differences has gained wide acceptance. That women's rights could be won only at the expense of those previously held by men does not seem to be either fair or reasonable, but this has become a tenet or motherhood issue for feminists as well as a myriad of other social libertarians. It was right to unburden women, but it is difficult to believe that men have to be emasculated in the process. The English author Charles Buxton (1823–71) wrote that "no man can do right unless he is good, wise, and strong," an observation that would appear to undermine the argument that a weak man makes for a freed woman. In fact, the argument against androgyny rests on the obvious: it becomes a completely unnatural state of affairs when men cannot be men and women cannot be women. A man who is taught that he should neither feel nor respond to the impulse of his manliness will never become the individual he is capable of becoming, without regard to either rightness or wrongness, goodness, wisdom, or strength. It is important that we know this. It is more important that we ensure that our sons know it as well.

## ORIENTATION TO MALENESS

One way to conceptualize the problem is to borrow terms like "orientation" and "position" from the Personologists. Cochran (1978a) tells us that position can be defined as identity, or perhaps role or status, and that becoming oriented means positioning oneself within some larger scheme, that is, "a definable place in an intelligible situation" (p. 7). When we use these terms, it is clear that when an individual is unsure of his identity, it is almost certain that he will be unable to assign to himself either role or persona. The recognition that the experiences and the interactions of the formative years are the only base from which positive self-regard can develop underscores the importance of ensuring that appropriate role models are available to youthful males. The role model for the very young male will continue to be the father, an uncle, or an older brother since propinquity appears to be a principal determining factor. In later years the young male will likely look beyond the borders of his immediate environment to seek out an appropriate model, but the degree to which he will be successful depends to a large measure on his earlier experiences. Identifying with the attitudes and the characteristics of masculinity is a series of developmental tasks that must be learned, arguably the earlier the better. The young male freely chooses from those attitudes and those characteristics that seem most reasonable to him, rejecting those attitudes and those characteristics that for one reason or another do not fit either his style or his personality. Those qualities that are demonstrated by the role model he has come to believe is most significant to him will tend to filter out the excesses of other models he may see around him, and in due course he will build his own unique hierarchy of attitudes and characteristics that will distinguish his masculinity from those of his peers and associates. Of all the developmental tasks a man must accomplish throughout his life, none is more critical than orienting himself to his personal condition and positioning himself so that his situation and his philosophical perspective are in reasonable accord.

Not long ago the extended family provided an adequate number of role models. Johnson (1986) writes,

> A world built around the family was not utopian by any means; the family is a microcosm of the larger society, a stage to play out conflicts and struggles, many of which we now play out on a larger stage. But the family offered a more satisfactory place for this, one that encouraged cooperation and mutual support rather than competition and calculation of individual gain. (p. 123)

As well, the influence of adults in one's immediate environment tended to be greater simply because in this earlier period of time the influences of the outside world did not intrude to the extent that they do at present. And even when society began to change and brought about the physical distancing that in time resulted in the nuclear family, there were still role models at hand, within the immediate family to be sure, but also in the larger number of friends and neighbors that came to fill the void brought on by the break-up of the extended family. Still, it is important to note that the structure of both the extended and the nuclear family encouraged continuing self-assessment in a relatively protective milieu and thus promoted the kind of formal and informal networking that has been demonstrated to be a critical element in the development of healthy self-regard. Although these structures undoubtedly exaggerated to some degree the qualities and attitudes of masculinity, the good news was that male role models were firmly set in place. Stability eased the process whereby a boy could identify with a male from within his own family unit. It was anticipated that in time a boy would take on role models from outside his own family; yet the entire process was a gradual one that developed over an extended period and in pace with the youth's emergence into adulthood.

Competition was encouraged because it was understood to be a useful way of determining one's capabilities, and for this purpose contests were arranged so that winners as well as losers might be identified. However, the other side of that particular coin was that neither winning nor losing was as important as the actual decision to compete. This is not to suggest that those who lost did not feel pain at losing or that those who won did not feel pleasure at winning; what it does suggest is that those who did not win profited from their loss and renewed their spirit with a determination that next time they would do better. This is a general statement to be sure,

and without doubt individuals suffered because they could not successfully compete. But on balance, more men were probably helped than were
hurt. It is also likely that those who were harmed in one way or another
had not been given the appropriate perspective from which to view their
participation.

It is interesting to contrast this viewpoint with the one currently in vogue
that describes competition of any kind in sinister terms. Young men as
well as small boys are now warned to avoid placing themselves in contest
with each other because somehow or other it is wrong to have some win
while others lose. It is difficult to understand this particular logic, primarily
because a sensible rationale that could support it is never really advanced,
other than that competition is simply not the democratic way of doing
things. One (possibly) unforeseen result has been a move away from open
and friendly competition. Competition, even in high school, has become
rigid and institutionalized; it is pursued for its own end rather than as the
means to an end. As professionals, a small number of really gifted athletes
are trained to a high level, sometimes drugged to a high level as well. They
are paraded out to perform feats of competition for the masses, not terribly
unlike the gladiators of the Roman Empire. Like the performers that they
really are, they earn enormous sums of money for what they do. Like
prostitutes, they are paid for their performance. When they compete well,
they receive the applause of the masses. When they do not, they are
discarded. And it is really quite that simple!

## THE MISUSE OF LINGUISTICS

In contemporary Western society, concepts as well as the words used
to explain them undergo frequent and dramatic shifts in meaning. At times
the transition is evolutionary in that the word or concept undergoes a
moderate change in meaning or shade of meaning, but at other times the
transition is revolutionary in that the meaning is significantly altered or
perhaps becomes a diametric opposite. It is clearly possible that most
words and concepts become altered either in the evolutionary or the
revolutionary sense owing to some kind of perceived need for change, but
it is also clear that meanings can also be deliberately altered. "All propaganda," wrote Adolf Hitler, "must be popular, and its intellectual level
must be adjusted to the most limited intelligence among those it is
addressed to. Consequently, the greater the mass it is intended to reach,
the lower its purely intellectual level will have to be" (1971, p. 180). To
be successful, the message must be simple, addressed to a specific popu-

lation, and repeated over and over. Propagandists of all hues and political persuasions have used the formula to varying degrees of success.

Carden (1974) details how the formula was put to use by activists within the feminist movement:

> The use of . . . "man hating" expressions like "male chauvinist pig" and "man as the oppressor" has disturbed many people. When first introduced, the terms were used by a few women to insult unsympathetic males. Within a short time however they became accepted as neutral concepts, used by all but the most conservative feminists as an efficient means of communication. (p. 51)

A majority of men would probably not agree that these terms have become enshrined in the language as nothing more than neutral concepts. The epithets were hurtful when first used, and remain hateful to this day. It is not necessary to argue that damage was done either to the individual male or to a collective male psyche, because such an argument would be beside the point. On the other hand, one has to question the stability of the person or group that tears down in order to build. And, if they were unstable then, what about now? Perhaps there is hope that this kind of after-the-fact rationalization will serve as a peace offering enabling bridge-building between a growing men's movement and a women's movement found wanting in sensitivity and goodwill. In point of fact, if bridge-building is the objective, the mea culpas can be the foundation. Still what has been done cannot be undone; what has been said cannot be unsaid. The use of offensive and confrontational rhetoric was an important part of a strategy designed to place men on the defensive. The strategy worked, perhaps too well, in that it introduced an unwelcome degree of conflict into gender interaction. The extent to which they were influenced depended on factors as diverse as level of consciousness or the kind of work they did, but both men and women discovered that relations between the sexes had become transformed almost overnight. The fundamental consequence was that attitudes toward men underwent remarkable change, a change that large numbers of males could not understand or easily adjust to. Part of the problem was an unsophisticated population not tuned into the way events come about, as in Bryce's observation that "opinion does not merely grow, it is also made" (1966, p. 17); but by far the larger part was that men generally were locked into attitudes that were as comfortable as they were time worn.

For an extended period of time a coordinated campaign of propaganda has been directed against the concept of masculinity in general, the individual man in particular, and most importantly the system of values that has served as the traditional bond between the individual and society. The campaign has celebrated the sensitive and intuitive qualities of womankind. Weisstein (1976) wrote that "the problem with insight, sensitivity, and intuition is that they can confirm for all times the biases that one started out with" (p. 94), and this is what much feminist rhetoric has been about. Clearly, ideological or societal positions that emerge from distorted logic are going to be convoluted, or worse. The truly awful aspect of the situation is that the reasonable has been made to appear unreasonable— for instance, the opening of a car door an attempt at power and control, the logic being that opening the door is a reference to the powerlessness of women and their need for men to be around to do things for them. In fact, a lot of feminist rhetoric appears to have been written by folk who fall into Toffler's (1971) category of "super simplifier," defined as the individual who "invests every idea he comes across with universal relevance."

De Rougemont (1966) explained that the superstition of our time "expresses itself in a mania for equating the sublime with the trivial and for mistaking a merely necessary condition for a significant cause" (p. 61). And inevitably the number and kind of causes vying for attention range from the sublime to the ridiculous, with promotion ranging along the same spectrum. Thus one can find environmentalists spraying paint on fur-bearing animals and demonstrators for peace wreaking havoc. It is some-what beside the point that paint reduces the animal's ability to withstand temperature change or that violence is the polar opposite of tranquillity! The cause takes on an importance of its own, and damn the consequences. One would think that verbal overkill could deflect the focus from the principal issue, but in fact it doesn't seem to work that way. The sideshow becomes the circus, a situation that in effect characterizes feminist rhetoric. This does not mean that the rhetoric has been ineffective. Quite the contrary. Their voices have been heard; the message has gained wide endorsement. As luck would have it, men are fortunate that the accusations from time to time have bordered on the intolerable, because overkill could conceivably have lessened the impact. Even so, and like activists whatever the cause, feminists displayed great skill when wielding the tools of the propagandist. As a consequence, a great deal of attention has centered on the need for females to become free from household slavery, very little on the male's need to be unyoked from the plow of job responsibility.

Feminists are not the only interest group who overstate their case to the point of losing sight of the original objective. Activists for the apparently endless assortment of minorities and causes seem to become more strident, more militant with every passing day, apparently without regard to either success or failure.

It might be helpful to liken activists to puppies that, once having learned to bark, continue to do so because it provides an activity as well as a purpose. Moreover, it is interesting that a common bond for activists of many kinds seems to emerge out of contempt for men and for constructs such as manliness and masculinity. The "they" that seem to be at the root of any problem is invariably related to some aspect of the male condition. Environmentalists scorn traditional pursuits such as hunting and fishing; peace activists concentrate on the male's alleged bellicosity. Feminists, along with gay and lesbian groups, complain about gender persecution to such an extent that anyone looking for a scapegoat can find one either in maleness or masculinity. Black males are too this, white males are too that, while Latinos or males of other ethnic origin are too something else again. In this new methodology, men are caricatured as unthinking, uncaring brutes determined to make life difficult for those who are not members of the club. It is curious, but those individuals who seem most energetic in promoting the myth are the very ones who argue that men have no justification for fighting back. They argue that the construct of male insensitivity is a given truth, central to the issue, and therefore cannot be a subject for discussion.

## THE BATTLE BETWEEN THE SEXES

The phrase "battle between the sexes" was probably coined by a stand-up comic making a joke about the way men and women react to each other. Later, it likely referred to one of those contests that caricatured the roles played by men and women. The competitions were somewhat unimaginative, but were thought to be funny because they tapped into the schadenfreude that beats in the heart of every person regardless of gender. A typical contest might have men baking pies, women chopping firewood. Of course one might argue that contests such as these were simple pleasures for simpler times, an age when people had the greater confidence in self that enabled them to laugh easily. In any case, all that is left now is the phrase itself, which no longer refers to good-natured rivalry but rather to the resounding echoes of a full-scale war.

In general, the fact that words and phrases can be skillfully used by the propagandist is the significant lesson to be learned. Contemporary man needs to learn to think more independently, most certainly not to be swayed by what he reads or sees or hears. He must identify his objectives as well as his interests and learn to march after them, and not fall in any lockstep cadence with peers who lack either his confidence or imagination or intellect. He needs to become keenly aware that things are not always the same as they seem, that it is as easy to believe a lie as the truth, and that it is sometimes very difficult to distinguish between what is real and what is not real. For example, no industrialized society has ever been able to commit the full extent of its resources to gender equality in the workplace. This has not happened, and for one reason or another it may never happen. But it takes a quantum leap in imagination to go from the fact that it hasn't happened to the conclusion that this is proof of a male conspiracy designed to keep women in their place. Arguments mustered to support unequal employment opportunities range from cherished beliefs rooted in tradition to those objections arising from specialized requirements of the work-place, including stamina and physical strength. Still, many women actually believe in the existence of a male plot, which of course is a testimony to the effective manner in which the feminist message has been packaged.

Bryce (1966) tells us that "everyone . . . is predisposed to see things in some one particular light by his previous education, habits of mind, accepted dogmas, religious or social affinities, and notions of his own personal interest. No event, no speech or article ever falls upon a perfectly virgin soil: the reader or listener is always more or less biased already" (p. 15). These words help us to understand why many women were prepared to believe in the existence of a male plot: the woman who has not met with bias or prejudice is very rare. A new level of truth built around a kernel of reality can be very appealing. One cannot deny that many women have been led to believe that employment discrimination is the inevitable result of male domination, so it is important for men to try to understand why they would be prepared to subscribe to this view. Yet there are few games on the go that cannot accommodate more than one player; however, to play the game one must learn the rules. And this is what this book is all about. For whatever the reason, men have watched the action from the sidelines when the truth of the matter is that they should have been on the playing field all the time. An oft repeated lie will become respected truth in due course, which in itself explains why men and masculinity have received such a trashing in recent years. It is time for the trashing to end. The best defense has long been recognized as the best offense, which in this case means that men will have to be prepared to be confrontational.

The psychology of the male is different from the psychology of the female. Men are neither nameless nor faceless, and cannot be characterized as either "they" or "them"; the psychology of the male is as individual as it is interactionist. Few behave either as the mindless children or sidestreet warriors they are frequently made out to be.

Ancient Greek conventional wisdom admonished man to know himself. The aim of this book is to give men an opportunity to become better acquainted with themselves, and with other men. To restore the balance, perhaps redress the grievance, it is not necessary either to attack or to counterattack. What is needed is knowledge of the issues, plus a keen interest in putting an end to male-bashing.

## 2

# Growing up Male

To make it easier for men to be men, we need a clearer masculine image. The ideal is not easy to define, but we know we want neither bookworms nor ape-men, neither predators nor sissies. Obviously we require few cave men because we no longer inhabit caves. Still, we need tough and courageous men—men who are also men of reason, tolerance, learning and good will. The shortage of male heroes and the entry into this vacuum of Minstrels, Musicians, Beatles, Rolling Stones—as well as an assortment of demented anti-heroes— makes it hard to personalize for the young any ideals of masculinity we may share.

—Patricia Sexton Cayo,
*The Feminized Male*

Words are the building blocks of language. Good use of body language helps get the message across, but words determine the degree of personal effectiveness. Words are used to win friends or to gain influence; they may also be used to keep people at a distance or enemies off guard. The propagandist uses words to inform or to disinform, to enlighten as well as to obfuscate. The individual skilled in language arts has the ability to convince the listener that white is black or that black is white, as well as points in between. Generally, men are better at body language than they are at words.

Acculturation processes have worked to firm up the belief that a person who speaks well or pays close attention to the way language is used is elitist, a description that can be the mark of Cain in a society that pretends to venerate egalitarianism. Precisely because people do not want to be considered elitist, a significant change has come about in the way people are constrained to think and act. There seems to be an attraction for the lowest common denominator, a topsy-turvy place where learning is devalued and grossness esteemed. It is our understanding of the truth rather than the truth itself that makes us free.

In all abuses of language, what is at stake is nothing less than the power to make distinctions. The phrase "a vital distinction" may be a cliché, but in one sense it is never an exaggeration. All distinctions are vital, because the ability to make distinctions is critical. The fates of individuals and of nations can and do swing on the hairbreadth difference between sentiment and sentimentality, heroism and heroics, misfortune and compulsion. Language is the tool of the distinction-making process, the sense wherein all the other senses mingle. To keep it as sharp and tough and service-bright as surgical steel is the first requisite of lucid thought (Pindell, 1983, p. 50).

## THE FEMINIST AGENDA

Blurring gender differences has always been a main objective on the feminist agenda. Taken at face value, blurring should not have emerged as a conceptual problem for either men or women. It seems likely that a strategy based more on reason and less on confrontation could have won broad support, from men as well as women. The differences between men and women have narrowed as a matter of course: role definitions that made reasonable sense in the eighth or sixteenth century, even the nineteenth, are nonfunctional in the twentieth. To be sure, technological advancements have brought dramatic change in the way most of us go about earning our daily bread. While the technological revolution was successful in marginalizing physical strength as a factor in the workplace, massive changes in social thinking encouraged women to compete for jobs from which they were previously excluded. Together, the revolution in technology and the revolution in social thinking combined to bring about an era in which radical change could have come easily to the workforce. However, change without confrontation was not to be. Whatever the reason, female activists opted for revolutionary rather than evolutionary change. It is fair to say that men were initially surprised and caught off their guard by a propaganda blitz that characterized them as insensitive brutes. Feminist literature avoided discussion of the obvious; that is, if unfeeling men were completely in charge of the business and professional world, who engineered the technological and social revolutions? The point is that men were never as adamantly opposed to women's rights issues as they were made out to be: it is a certainty that had the majority of men been opposed, any advance in the status quo would have been glacial. It is probably closer to the truth to suggest that women's rights were for most men a nonissue.

Feminism was built on an unfailing belief in androgyny (Bem, 1974), a concept that continues to raise passions on both sides of the gender divide. Androgyny promotes a sexist agenda because it encourages the belief that feminine qualities are always praiseworthy, those of the male never. Page (1987) notes that androgyny "has drawn criticism on the grounds that it remains a highly evaluative concept, in effect another sex-role stereotype in which the traditional notions of masculinity and femininity are retained (maybe even promoted)" (p. 58). Page observes that writers like Graham and Stark-Adamec (1978) and Pyke (1981), want to "leave androgyny behind . . . and proceed to build the case for . . . sex role transcendence, in which sex-based evaluative concepts and biases would be absent" (p. 58). If transcendence implies recognizing that differences exist but that ways must be found so that neither men nor women can be discriminated against, it is clear that this is the direction in which society must move. Mature human beings do not take offense at one another's differences.

Feminist propaganda has enjoyed a level of success far beyond what it should have. This statement is difficult to defend because it swims against the current of populist thought. In large measure the literature was successful because the time for change had arrived and the basic message tapped into a reservoir of public goodwill. The problem arises not with the basic message of equality, but rather with the excesses of the messengers who delivered it.

Truth is the first casualty in propaganda.

## DETERMINING THE ISSUES

Although the number of issues that appear to complicate relations between the sexes seems to be infinite, in fact there are only two of concern for men. In the first instance, men need to become keenly aware that feminists really do view the battle between the sexes as an actual battle: there is no good nature in the rivalry. Second, although men should try not to be confrontational, meeting challenge with challenge and hostility with hostility, confrontation should not be avoided at all costs. Trying to keep the peace by remaining silent has not worked: it can be argued that this lack of strategy has on the whole been counterproductive. Takacs (1983) noted that "for many years women have enjoyed the moral superiority that comes from being recognized as the victims in the acrimonious battle of the sexes" (p. 71). Operating from this high moral ground gave feminists the edge; they were able to argue the righteousness of their cause and make men feel guilty at the same time. Takacs warns feminists that the tables are about to be turned.

> Across Canada and the United States men are going on the offensive, claiming they are victims of sex discrimination and challenging the sexist privileges that they say are enjoyed by women. As with their female counterparts, male liberationists are fired by anger and indignation. They are tired of bringing home the bacon while the women live off their efforts and monopolize the emotional rewards of raising children. They will no longer sit by timorously while divorce courts automatically grant custody of their sons and daughters to their former wives. (1983, p. 71)

The important lesson to be learned is that there is a new reality out there, and that men will have to find individual as well as collective ways to deal with it. Men will have difficulty dealing with this new awareness because in a general sense they are not prepared to accept the notion of woman-as-enemy. Even today, it seems clear that the overwhelming majority of men are not persuaded to take feminist rhetoric seriously. The average fellow laughs, at times with scorn in his voice, and sometimes dismisses all feminists as lesbian. This is not to say that all women are enemies. On the other hand, since large numbers have selectively bought into the feminist agenda of categorizing all men as insensitive clods, the average man might learn to be a bit more wary.

## DEVALUATION OF TRADITIONAL MASCULINE VALUES

Feminist rhetoric aims to devalue traditional values of masculinity, but the degree to which the effort has been successful is difficult to measure. Where the effect on the mainstream of masculine thinking is concerned, it is doubtful that such a mainstream even exists. While it may be reasonable to believe that some men have undergone some change in attitude, it is unlikely that any large number of men have been persuaded to believe they are personally guilty for the way women were treated in earlier periods of human history.

Although feminists have emerged as the new leaders of the anti-male crusade, what they are saying is not truly all that new. Epithets of the "male chauvinist pig" type have been coined in recent years, and with repeated usage have become integrated into the language. Expressions such as these are used in order to shock, but more importantly they become slogans in the feminist rhetoric. They are meant to hurt as well. And sometimes they do. It is difficult to believe that any individual, man or woman, would feel good while being called names. Feminists are wont to believe that men have to accept slings and arrows as part of the penance for the many injustices done to women throughout the ages. It is more likely that men have not reacted because of the age-old belief that men must not fight women. In fact, men have been immobilized because of historical precedent. Clearly it is time for men to become less complacent.

## THE IMPACT OF RELIGION

On the surface, the feminist philosophy of liberation appears to be the polar opposite of a religious tradition that places men in high position in church, state, family, and social hierarchies. Several of the Protestant sects in Christianity have ordained women into their ministry, but commitment to a male clergy by the Roman Catholic Church as well as some of the fundamentalist Protestant denominations remains unchanged. Female participation in church leadership does not appear to be much of an issue in other world religious traditions.

From the beginning, world religions have centered on an all-male clergy. This same tradition elevated men above women, directed women to obey their husbands, and otherwise worked to ensure woman's role as helpmate for the male. The church became a reflection of the larger society: it grew to be patriarchal because the larger society was patriarchal. A patriarchal society burdened men with responsibility; a patriarchal religion added to the burden.

For the most part, contemporary religious thought does not reflect the changes that have taken place in the larger society. The central problem for the established church seems to be one of remaining credible in the face of dramatic change. The basic problem is that if the guiding principle for religion is revealed truth, how is it possible to change that which has been revealed? Thus, if truth is a constant, how can it be altered? The problem will not be easy to resolve.

On the surface, there does not appear to be an anti-male bias in religion. However, a bias does exist and it is fascinating to liken the anti-male bias that fuels the feminist movement with the orientation bias of a patriarchal denomination such as the Roman Catholic Church. While the consequences of malediction may not be at all dissimilar from those of benediction, the important distinction seems to be that feminists target the group while the church targets the individual. Viewed thus, it is easily seen that it is the fear of what the individual man might do if left to his own devices that has brought about the exquisitely detailed moral, ethical, and philosophical codes that have influenced the direction of Christianity. For the most part, one assumes these codes grow out of the hierarchy's fear that the clergy would not be able to remain celibate without strict guidelines in place.

The Roman Catholic Church, in particular, remains uncompromisingly patriarchal. There is no provision whatsoever for women to work their way into senior positions of religious leadership. On the surface this attitude would seem to reflect, or perhaps to continue, the Jewish system of the patriarchal family. The respect that the man received, whatever his calling in life, was based on love as well as honor, and was accorded to the father of a household as well as to a revered rabbi or an accomplished cantor. The love as well as the honor was an uncomplicated religious truth that flourished in Judaism.

From its Semitic beginnings, how and when the Christian church began to build an anti-male bias into its religious structure is a subject more appropriately addressed by an ecclesiastical historian. The moral and ethical philosophy that Christ taught was congruent with religious thought of the day. Some, but not all, of his teachings were revisionary. However, in the very important respect of leadership, which came to be called priesthood, he was not revisionist at all. Women were not called, only men. Andreas (1971) noted that "virtually all major religions of the world include strong commandments to the two genders to act in a manner consistent with traditional patriarchal social arrangements" (p. 96), and the church that came to be called Christian is no exception.

From the beginning the Christian church has endeavored to build a monolithic theocracy. As religious law emerged from social custom, complicated formulas evolved that in point of fact fixed the punishment for the crime. In time, the church made it possible for the sinner to know the consequences of the transgression before the action was undertaken. A cynic might argue that the exercise of free will was in effect nothing other than a matter of deciding between action and consequence, or pleasure versus punishment.

The principal concern for the early church was propagation of the faith, which was in truth more or less what Christ had ordered his apostles to do. Propagation of the faith would necessarily involve a great deal more than converting the Jews and other assorted unbelievers. Propagation of the faith also meant ensuring that the sons and daughters of the faithful would remain faithful, and that they would marry and produce offspring who would also be faithful and who would in due course produce offspring who would be faithful, and so forth. Considered independently of all other mandates that the Christian church came to believe as part of its mission, propagating the faith had to be considered the first priority.

### Monogamy in Marriage

The monogamous marriage as a social institution existed centuries before the establishment of the Christian church as a social force. It is likely that the early fathers of the church elevated marriage to the status of a sacrament because they well understood that growth depended on stability. Men were expected to marry and remain married as long as they lived, and moreover were made responsible for either the success or failure of the union. The man who married was provided a natural outlet for his sexual appetite, making it quite unnecessary for him to go elsewhere for gratification. Because marriage provided him with the outlet in the Christian tradition, it became a serious transgression to look elsewhere for sexual gratification. In due course, legal restraint followed religious constraint. The requirement that a man must marry tended to bring about the kind of stable society in which the church could prosper, but the more important consideration was that in the logical course of events children born from the union would be reared within the bosom of the church. For the most part, the church prospered because it took control of the institution of marriage. Interestingly, a married clergy fell into disfavor with church fathers because some priests found it difficult to reconcile responsibilities to the two institutions they were trying to serve. It might be argued as well that some could easily have come to a belief that family responsibility outweighed pastoral responsibility, which one suspects would not have met with favor by the church fathers.

It is not at all certain that the institution of marriage will survive the stresses and strains placed on it by the social currents of the latter half of the twentieth century. As people moved out of a predominantly agrarian society, the strains on the institution of marriage began to increase. In the earlier decades of the twentieth century the taboos against breaking marriage vows worked to keep most men and women committed to their married state, but a general breakdown of marriage as an institution began to occur in the years immediately following World War II. It is likely that the institution will survive in one form or another simply because formalized commitment to someone you love does have strong appeal, but the covenant will increasingly become more social and less religious.

From its earliest days the Christian religion has advocated completely different and separate roles for men and for women. In essence, man was the provider and woman was provided for. When the man took this obligation seriously, it meant that he would be conscientious in his work ethic and his wife would be well looked after. Conversely, when for one reason or another the man did not provide, his woman was not well looked after. This is a simplistic overview of a complicated social issue, but in point of fact the bottom line was that the welfare of the woman was determined by the success her husband had in coping with his world of work, regardless of what that world of work might have been. Again, and whether it was a plot or not, the woman's awareness that her well-being depended on her ability to marry a man who would support her in whatever style she deemed appropriate was a certain guarantee that women would support the efforts of the church to ensure the stability of marriage as an institution.

## Homophobia

Insofar as church leadership was concerned, there was yet another compelling reason for men to marry. The church's concern with homosexuality was not published widely nor even greatly discussed, but in fact the fathers of the early church had to be keenly aware that monks and priests alike lived and worked in the kind of all-male environment that has been known to give rise to situational homosexuality. As a result of this concern the early church fathers pronounced homosexuality a sin against God as well as man, and in the course of events unleashed the wave of revulsion that has imprecisely come to be termed homophobia. For those who were not bound to a religious life of service and sacrifice, St. Paul preached that marriage was the only acceptable outlet for a man's sexual appetite. Married or not, men were told that their sexual urges could lead them into a state of eternal damnation. Laymen were provided with natural sexual outlets in the person of their wives: those who took up a religious vocation were made to take vows of chastity.

Earlier societies had endorsed or tolerated homosexual relationships. Sparta fielded an army that was largely homosexual. Other Greek city-states encouraged young men to learn from the old. When learning became entangled with expressions of personal devotion, as it often did, it was considered to be one of the many ways for bonding to come about. In retrospect it does seem quite possible that the homophobia that came to play so large a part in the morality of Christendom grew out of an unawareness of the dynamics of bonding. It must be remembered that the apostles were not men of learning: this is no attempt to indict, but rather to explain that the early church fathers were simple fishermen whose followers were also simple folk.

The Eastern cultures, and especially those that espouse arranged marriages, seemed to appreciate the flowering of bonding from respectful affiliation with either sex. People from these cultures recognized that married love begins with the bond set into place by propinquity; they also seemed to understand that homosexuality is not a consequence of same-sex bonding. Because it flowed from the same cultural wellspring, early Christian tradition would likely have been equally tolerant of bonding. However, concern that the sexual well-being of an increasingly celibate clergy might be at risk from bonding relationships led to a new kind of tradition—that of doctrinaire homophobia. Then, as Christian teachings began to influence all of the Western world, homophobia became rampant in Western Europe. It may be considered strange that homophobia never became as strong in the actual birthplace of Christianity, that is, the Middle East, but the reason for this is most likely to be found in the heterogeneous religious mix that has always populated the area. But in Western Europe, where homophobia became solidly entrenched as an article of faith, men had to develop new styles of behavior in relating to other men. Above all, the manner in which one man could relate to another man had to be completely free from affect, or feeling. As a result, aggressive behavior was routinely encouraged in the youthful male simply because it was believed that aggressiveness could mask feelings of affection (even when they were present). Vance (1990) is more direct when he writes, "men in general are not taught to love anyone very well. We are raised as warriors to the detriment of our other psychic parts. Warriors do not love. They fight, they fuck, they follow directions unerringly." The characterization is simplistic, disturbingly insensitive, and to a degree accurate. Seidler (1989) argues that the language men use is forged for self-assertion, and that it is the way we talk to one another that makes it harder for men to form close and intimate relationships. Men in therapy are sometimes puzzled by the amount of attention directed to content and process of communication.

> Heterosexual men often have an experience of feeling locked inside themselves, unable to share themselves even with those to whom they feel closest. Often this is a desperate silence, which might explain the attraction of more expressive forms of therapy for men who have got involved in consciousness-raising groups. This gives some kind of experiential background to people's involvement in therapy which already challenges the ways men in particular learn to distance

ourselves from our own experience through humour, cynicism and
irony, so that we never risk ourselves. We cannot be hurt. We learn
to make ourselves invulnerable. We learn not to care too much or too
deeply about anything, or else we throw ourselves intensively into
activities. (Seidler, p. 104)

Today, the majority of adult men in the Western world still bear the
scars of homophobic programming in the distancing that characterizes
their relationship with other men. It is quite acceptable of course for male
children to have male playmates and for teen-age boys to have other
teen-age boys as buddies, or good friends, especially if their friendship
centers on athletics. But adult men are expected to put distance between
themselves and other males. Again, male athletes of any age are not bound
by the rules, presumably because competition bears the acceptable stamp
of aggressiveness. In conforming to the expectations of the homophobic
society that surrounds them, the majority of men have internalized the
attitude to the extent that they are unaware that their behavior toward other
males is truly outside the realm of the normal. More often than not, any
degree of intimate friendship with another male is cause for concern, if
not guilt-provoking. In *A Strange Breed of Cat*, the character Mike put it
this way: "Men have great difficulty relating to each other simply because
sex is in the way. You get so afraid that just because you like some other
guy so damn much that some damn fool is going to come along and call
you homo" (Schoenberg, 1975, p. 144). In any balancing of the scales, all
of the good works of Christianity and all the sacrifices of its martyrs have
to be weighed against the harm done to men by its homophobic stance.

## EGALITARIANISM

Egalitarianism in its simplest terms describes a philosophy that advocates a doctrine of equal political, economic, and legal rights for everyone.
It has come to be something of a flag-and-motherhood issue, and those
who are not one hundred percent for are considered to be one hundred
percent against. The hard reality is that there is little room for compromise
between the human rights activist and the individual who questions
whether equality can always be legislated into place.

A philosophical position inevitably brings on a selectivity in vision; in
that sense, philosophers who espouse principles of egalitarianism are not
different from those embracing differing systems of belief. Yet, because
it is a relatively unsophisticated system, egalitarianism has a standard of
popular acceptance that in numbers far exceeds the more intricate philos-
ophies. The face of society has changed as the basic principles of egalitar-

ianism have become woven into the fabric of cherished folklore. Mostly for the better, but not always.

The problem with egalitarianism resides not in its dogma, but rather in too literal an interpretation of the dogma itself. For example, despite Jefferson's pronouncement that all men are created equal, genetic differences do exist; and these genetic differences enable some men to excel beyond the competencies of others. In addition, regardless of rhetoric, men are more able in some activities while women are more able in others. This is the fact of the matter, and the differences will remain for the majority of men and for the majority of women regardless of how the balance might be weighted in favor of one or the other. To attempt to argue that the differences do not exist, or that they exist solely because of cultural imprinting, is farcical and represents a gross distortion of what egalitarianism is all about. Males and females have been engineered with biological givens that cause them to be psychologically different, so in a purely genetic sense true equality can never be completely achieved. Further, although it is completely reasonable to argue for a level playing field, chalk simply cannot be made from cheese. As far back as 1966, Brenton commented that "the great outpouring of words about the contemporary American women these past few years has made it seem as though the male either had no problems or didn't count enough to have them aired" (p. 13). The outpouring has long since turned into a tidal wave, the basic message seeming to be that the traditional pattern of sex role differentiation is no longer useful, that it now serves only to lock men and women into stifling conformity. Goldberg (1973) makes the point that "biology can never justify refusing any particular option, but it does explain universal sexual differences in behavior and institutions where cultural and environmental explanations cannot" (p. 146).

There have been a number of attempts to balance out inequalities brought about by gender differences: in point of fact, American legislators have written and enacted legislation that seeks to compensate for inequalities brought about by gender. In theory, egalitarianism is appealing; in practice, it does not work. Indeed, an unbridled egalitarianism has the potential to destroy the modern industrial state for the simple reason that workers generally are not willing to support those who elect not to work. The indications are many that this is beginning to happen in several of the welfare states of Northern and Western Europe. The public school system provides another example of the kinds of problems that arise when efforts to ensure full measures of equality are set into place. Social engineering designed to bring egalitarian principles into the schools has degraded education standards: the curricula in primary and secondary education have been so watered down for the underachiever that the average student is no longer challenged. The result has been a steady deterioration of the system, marked particularly by severe underdevelopment of students' educational potential. In its wake, the planners left an alarming number of young people in a state of undisturbed ignorance.

## THE WOMEN'S LIBERATION MOVEMENT

In terms of stridency, few can match those who preach the gospel of the women's liberation movement. Every community, small as well as large, seems to have a cadre of radical feminists available to seize on any issue that can bring their cause to the attention of the media. Protesting here, haranguing there, the feminist agenda is drafted for maximum visibility.

Writing in 1970, Bednarik noted that "the impotent anger smouldering in our society has long been reflected in angry literature which hits out blindly and violently in all directions, providing an outlet, in a sort of psychological striptease, in stories of monomaniacal suffering, in novels, poems of protest, satiric cabarets, and the theatre of the absurd" (p. 27). In most respects these words capture the spirit of the feminist rhetoric that fuels the women's movement because the objective is to portray men, maleness, and masculinity in mean and spiteful terms. The format follows the artfully crafted storyline that women have routinely suffered outrageous excesses at the hands of men. There is the suggestion that, once women have been liberated from their chains, they will become invincible and will be able to put an end to nationalism, nuclear proliferation, and all the other problems that men have visited on the human species. The message seems to be that the kinder and gentler wisdom that women possess will ensure that personkind will at long last set foot on the actual road to paradise lost.

Militancy for the sake of militancy seems to characterize much of the feminist posturing, but perhaps it is not feigned at all. Sustaining enthusiasm for an incredibly broad range of issues is probably sufficient cause for distemper.

### The Issue of Psychological Emasculation

It is an article of feminist faith that for woman to become strong, man must become weak. The argument is truly basic to the distorted reasoning that in order for women to gain power, men must be forced to yield. The notion that yielding must take place applies in equal measure to the gender, to the individual, and to the construct of maleness or masculinity. Haggarty

(1975) notes instances of homosexual rape in prison where the intent is one of robbing an inmate of his masculinity, and in the process ensuring his removal from any position of power in the inmate hierarchy. Rape of one man by another is a particularly devastating personal assault, frequently causing the kind of psychological emasculation that leads to self-devaluation. But psychological emasculation is the name of the game insofar as feminist rhetoric is concerned: They may be reluctant to spell out the objective in so explicit a manner, but it is well past the time when men need to become aware that repeated denunciations of maleness, manliness, and masculinity by feminists and those whom Roszak and Roszak (1969) have described as male allies represent a conscious, deliberate, and well-planned assault on maleness and masculinity. Indeed, Millett (1970) affirms the intent when she writes that "a sexual revolution would bring the institutions of patriarchy to an end, abolishing both the ideology of male supremacy and the traditional socialization by which it is upheld in matters of status, role, and temperament" (p. 62). Eisenstein (1981) has argued, "the major purpose of patriarchy, besides actualizing its system of power, is mystifying the basis of this power so that it cannot be recognized by the oppressed" (p. 223). Clearly, the "they" responsible for setting patriarchy in place did their homework well: mystifying and obscuring at one and the same time is quite an accomplishment.

Physiological and biological givens have weighted characteristics like strength and endurance in favor of the male, but other characteristics such as stamina and longevity appear to be weighted in favor of the female. In a psychological sense women have long had the edge over men because the patterns of socialization that evolved from patriarchy encouraged women to be manipulative. Because women learned to manipulate men successfully, it is fair to say that in a psychological sense they have long held the trump card. Indeed, Vilar (1972) suggests that men are enslaved and that women have emerged as the oppressors. Such a view presents the diametric opposite of feminist rhetoric, and clearly challenges constructs both traditional and cherished. The bottom line is that successful relationships between the sexes can only be forged through mutual respect and understanding. The well-cherished notion that women can gain rights only by robbing men of theirs has to be put to rest.

Relationships between men and women will improve because it will be recognized that each must provide an equal measure of support to the other. For their part, men must learn to appreciate and accept that women have come to see themselves quite differently. Many of these new perceptions are appropriate, others are not at all useful, and some have been so distorted by disinformation as to become ludicrous. As well, men have to become aware of the guilt trip that feminists are trying to lay on them. Men as well as women were abused by the patriarchal system, the difference being either of kind or degree. Finally, men must be very careful not to get locked into a continuing battle with feminists. It is clear that until now men have been on the losing side of the public relations battle. In a broad sense men have been maneuvered into positions that required defending, or atoning, or apologizing: sometimes all three, often a combination. Men must set about articulating a philosophical perspective that sends out a clear message that the days of abuse have come to an end.

## MAN, MALENESS, MANLINESS, AND MASCULINITY

It is difficult to understand why it has become so important to replace the generic word "man" with the vacuous word "person." In part it might be explained as yet another phenomenon of the times in which black becomes white, evil is made into good, and right becomes wrong. The better explanation is that the purge has taken on a life of its own: women who display little or no interest in other women's issues have shown enthusiasm for this one. Professional associations, particularly those with high percentages of female members, started the practice of referring to chairmen as chairpersons. From those modest beginnings, the practice has snowballed.

The practice also grates. In point of fact, no individual deserves to be neutered. It is foolish for men to be called "persons"; it is equally foolish for women to be called "persons." Chairman is generic; but if a woman objects, let her be termed "chairwoman." Or "chair," for that matter. It's all right for an individual to become neutered if he or she wants it that way, but asexuality should not be forced on anyone. Protagonists claim they do battle with a sexist bias in language, and in their zeal add gems like "waitperson" and "fisherperson" to the living language. In the process, a new level in comedy has been achieved.

A question arises: What or who is "man"? At its functional best, the word is gender-descriptive. In its most literal sense, it becomes the word that is used to describe a human being when the gender of that human being is either not relevant or somewhat beside the point. One example, the man in the moon; a second, chairman. The plural of "man" is used in the same way as its singular counterpart. The distinctions are not difficult to grasp, and the simple fact is that for hundreds of years people who spoke English were sufficiently aware of the nuances.

Other words are more clear insofar as gender identification is concerned.

For example, the word "masculine" describes attitudinal and behavioral characteristics that are considered appropriate to the biological inheritance of the male. In this same spirit, the word "manly" is used to describe attitudes and behaviors that are judged to be appropriate to the civil, or social, or gentle man. These words, along with others such as "manliness" and "masculinity," suggest stylized attitudinal and behavioral codes of conduct considered appropriate for the male.

An understanding of what constitutes masculine behavior or how a man should lead his life in order to be considered manly changes with the time and with the place. What is masculine on one socioeconomic level may not be considered masculine on another level. In actual fact there is an urban definition as well as a rural one, and a national definition to be considered along with a regional one. An additional complication is the extent to which the mores of society have changed since meaning was given to words such as these. The great majority of men no longer hew wood or draw water, skills highly in demand for our male progenitors. Nor is the contemporary man expected to be the family's sole provider; yet a cultural lag has combined with entrenched attitudes to ensure that some men feel guilty if their wives work outside the home. Attempts have been made to define the new social reality from a male perspective, but more needs to be done or else Western society is going to become androgynous far sooner than anybody is really ready for it.

## 3

# Sex and Gender

Our society has been so inundated with psychoanalytic thinking that any dissatisfaction or conflict in personal and family life is considered to require solution on an individual basis. This goes well with the general American value stress on individualism, and American women have increasingly resorted to psychotherapy, the most highly individualized solution of all, for the answers to the problems they have as women. In the process the idea has been lost that many problems, even in the personal family sphere, cannot be solved on an individual basis, but require solution on a societal level by changing the institutional contexts within which we live.

—Alice S. Rossi,
*Equality Between the Sexes: An Immodest Proposal*

At one time it was possible to read clinical literature and be relatively certain that the information being presented would be reliable, factual, and of course objective. The certainty is no longer there, and much of the credit/blame for this can be attributed to feminist writers. Perhaps the explanation for this fall from professional grace can be traced to the influence of a popular press that over a period of time grew incapable of distinguishing between editorializing and news reporting. But perhaps not. The explanation could be simpler. It may simply be a matter of commitment bringing on tunnel vision. Takacs (1983) offers an explanation that varies slightly. She writes, "Equality—true equality—is such an emotional issue that few seem able to see beyond their own self-interest" (p. 71).

Why should men be concerned with what is happening in the clinical literature or indeed the popular press? Clearly it is beyond the power of most men to do much about what is written in either place. But having said that, we must add that what is written can also be monitored; this is important because when disinformation is not corrected, the larger risk is that it will be accepted as truth. Given that social attitudes grow out of the printed and spoken word, it is essential in the first instance that men become aware that newspapers and professional journals are being manipulated as never before, and in the second that men learn to do something about it. What a man can do about it naturally depends on what he has going for him. Some can refute, others can use their influence to restore a semblance of balance, others need only be aware.

Double-talk is generally couched in the most reasonable terms. At its effective best, the technique requires a writing style so caring and so sensitive as to blind the reader to the actual reason for the piece. The argument should be phrased in the most reasonable language, one point flowing artfully and logically into the next.

The aim is to obscure without appearing to obscure; to confuse without appearing to confuse. "Propaganda," as Ellul (1968) has noted, "must be familiar with collective sociological presuppositions, spontaneous myths, and broad ideologies" (p. 38). The propagandist uses the familiar, that is, the presupposition, the myth, or the ideology, as the base on which a new reality can be erected.

English and English (1958) define propaganda as "actions or expressions of opinion, by individuals or groups, that are deliberately designed to influence the opinions or actions of other individuals or groups" (p. 413). According to this definition, it is clear that a propaganda war directed against men and their masculinity has been waged in the past, is being waged in the present, and, unless it is stopped, will be waged in the future. Men are blamed for what they do, for what they did not do, and for whatever they may or may not do. According to the rhetoric, neither men nor men's deeds can ever be well intentioned, because everything that goes on can and will be interpreted subjectively. For the most part, men have underestimated the impact of all those who belittle or devalue the traditional trappings of maleness and masculinity. As unfortunate as that may be, the worst part is that most men are still not aware that a war is being waged against them.

## DEFINITION OF TERMS

We all thirst after the fountain of knowledge. Becoming well informed is a personal responsibility; narrowing the field of knowledge is one of personal choice. The problem is that the flow of information is limitless, what we are able to integrate finite. The individual who tries to remain up to date in all matters ends up knowing a little bit about a lot of things but not very much about any one of them. The areas that a person does choose define his/her family, work, and of course social parameters. But becoming well informed means more than selecting topics to read or subjects to study. It means reading well, speaking well, and listening well.

To read well, to speak well, to listen well requires attention to detail. In this day and time, the insidious "you know" is the most popular way to end a sentence. A first appraisal suggests that the user is too lazy to complete his sentence, but a second might ask "What's the big deal?" Well, the big deal is that this seemingly harmless little phrase tucked in at the end of a sentence invites, perhaps forces, the listener to form closure on whatever incomplete thought the speaker happens to be voicing. The obvious problem centers on congruence. In other words, how gifted is the listener at mind reading? If not mind reading, what is the statistical probability of building a complete data base from data that is incomplete? It is possible, even probable, that whether or not one fully grasps the intent of the speaker is relatively unimportant most of the time. This is another way of saying that most of what we say and most of what we hear is relatively unimportant. But habits, regardless of how they are formed, become ingrained and tend to generalize: the habit of careless speech is no exception to that general rule.

As important as it is to ensure that the thought is complete, it is probably even more important to ensure that others know the words used to express it. Words and terms must be defined, for the speaker as well as the listener, for propaganda relies on vague speech. In this context, it becomes necessary to define the several words that are central to an understanding of maleness and masculinity. The most appropriate use for the word "sex" is to differentiate between the specialized biological heritage that is either male or female. The word "gender" describes the cultural or psychological differences between the male and the female, those that are most commonly referred to as either masculine or feminine. The words "sex" and "gender" are sometimes used as if they were synonymous, or interchangeable. But they are not synonymous and are not necessarily related to one another.

A biological given can be altered only by surgery, but cultural or psychological givens can be altered by events as dissimilar as situational necessity, incidental learning, and/or brainwashing. "Gender identity," according to Money and Ehrhardt (1972), "is the sameness, unity and persistence of one's individuality as male or female (or ambivalent) in greater or lesser degrees, especially as it is experienced in self-awareness and behavior. Gender identity is the private experience of gender role and gender role is the public expression of gender identity" (p. 284). According to English and English (1958), gender "is a . . . synonym for sex wherever the sheer difference in physical structure between male and female is meant" (p. 221), and sex role "is the pattern of attitudes and behaviors that in any society is deemed appropriate to one sex rather than the other" (p. 498). If gender identity is the private experience of gender role, then it must be assumed that sex role identity is the private experience of sex role. Both identities, gender and sex role, grow out of perceptions formed from comparison of the real and ideal selves; and both are, of course, value judgments. These two identities form the concept of a sexual self. Schoenberg and Preston (1983) wrote that the way people develop their sexual self-concept is probably no different in substance from the manner in which they form their overall concept of self, but argued that "the subtleties of sex-role conditioning provide additional stumbling blocks" (p. 222). Finally, Lazarus and Folkman (1984) describe the concept of morale as "the way we feel about ourselves and the condition of our lives, and the extent to which we feel satisfaction or unhappiness" (p. 308).

## BIOLOGICAL INHERITANCE

According to Sandler, Myerson, and Kinder (1980), "psychosexual differentiation, or the formation of an individual's sexual identity, starts at conception and continues through early childhood. . . . The elements involved in the process of biological sexual differentiation are the genes, gonads, hormones, internal reproductive structures, and external genitalia" (p. 74). In her book *Males and Females*, Hutt (1972) tell us that "in fact, distinctively male and female development in the human being begins at the moment of conception" (p. 76). The genetic imprint of psychosexual differentiation begins when the male's sperm fertilizes the female's ova, and in a physiological sense, the primary sexual characteristics continue to develop as the fetus continues to grow. These primary characteristics do not suggest that male and female may be different: they ordain that they will be different. Duberman (1975) writes that "sex . . . is an ascribed social status referring to the biological difference between people. Males are born with male genitalia; females, with female genitalia. This is sex status —rarely misperceived, rarely alterable. Like other ascribed statuses, it is acquired at birth and is independent of skill, effort, or ability" (p. 26). Sex status is gender attribution, the base on which personality configurations such as gender role and gender identity are eventually built—or not built, whichever the case may be. Because of this, and for as long as they live, from the moment of conception until the instant of death, the male and the female will perceive their existence through this filter of psychosexual differentiation. The reproductive organs are homologous; that is, they develop from the same embryonic tissue. But differentiation antedates development, so in this way male and female may be said to be complementary. However, they are not the same, and this is the biological inheritance.

Sandler, Myerson, and Kinder (1980) noted that the biological emphasis of sexuality is usually attributed to Freud because (1) he recognized the importance of infantile sexuality, and (2) his explanation of psychosexual development focused on sexual drive, that is, the libido. But according to Kessler and McKenna (1978), "for Freud, the study of gender was essentially the study of gender roles. The problem was not how children learn that they are a particular gender, but rather (in contemporary terms) how do children develop the appropriate gender role—how and why do boys become masculine and girls become feminine?" (p. 88). Weitz (1977) argued that the differing reproductive roles for men and women were important in the shaping of male and female sexuality. She wrote, "When we consider sexuality as a biological backdrop for socialization throughout the life cycle, we must concentrate on the different meanings of sexuality for men and women" (p. 24). Finally, Garai and Scheinfeld (1968) have noted that "a substantial body of research evidence . . . has been accumulated to provide . . . the skeleton for an integrated theory of sex differences." Their research conclusions are invaluable building blocks in understanding the male's biological inheritance. These investigators list a total of fourteen conclusions, but the first four are of particular interest:

1. The male organism is inherently physically stronger, heavier, taller, more active, and more aggressive than the female organism.

2. The male organism is more susceptible to genetic defects and diseases and less resistant to most biological hazards than is the female organism.

3. The male organism matures much more slowly and for a much longer time than the female organism, achieving puberty from 1½ to 2½ years later and reaching full physiological and mental maturity approximately 3 to 5 years later in the twenties.

4. The much more prolonged maturation of boys from puberty to adulthood affords greater opportunity for the development of

physical skills. This prolonged development adds further to the inherent advantage of the male in strength, height, and weight, and increases the male superiority in sports, athletics, and physical tasks (p. 269).

It is clear that there will always be exceptions to these general statements. There have always been females who are physically stronger and heavier than the average male. Steinem (1972) would argue that the differences between men and women are cultural, not biological; and although Wesley and Wesley (1977) might concede some obvious and some not so obvious differences between males and females, their bottom line is that the psychological differences center mainly on the culturally established sex roles (p. 15). Chafetz (1974) answers the query, "Where does gender leave off and sex role begin?" by saying, "Given present evidence, no precise line between organism and environment, gender and role, can be drawn" (p. 4). Garai and Scheinfeld (1968) add the caveat that "the generalizations upon which this theory is based can be accepted only if one keeps in mind that we are dealing with identifiable averages derived from the study of males as a group and females as a group" (p. 269). Clearly there is a lot of semantic grasping.

During the period of pubescence, in the normal course of development, appearance of the secondary sexual characteristics will generally accentuate the difference between the sexes. In 1955, Money, Hampson, and Hampson observed that the assignment of sex at birth is the best predictor of the adult sex role, and it is in infancy that rapid physiological changes come about. The process of role differentiation may begin during this period, but pressures associated with learning/conforming seem to increase as the child grows older. The child learns those behaviors and those attitudes that are appropriate to his or her sex, and reinforcement comes about through a subtle yet complex system of rewards and punishments. The ability to differentiate leads to development of the sexual role, which when successfully integrated leads to acceptance of gender identity.

The several kinds of sex change operations can re-form genitalia, which are the primary sexual characteristic, and hormone injections to a large extent can marginalize the physical effects of the secondary characteristics. Such operations are of real value to individuals who believe that they are locked into a physical body not consonant with sexual identity. Still, the number of people who may require such an operation is thought to be small. These include those who may have been misidentified at birth, as previously noted by Chafetz (1974), as well as those who for one reason or another have not been able to come to terms with either gender identity or sex role.

## THE PSYCHOLOGICAL IMPRINT
## OF SEX AND GENDER

The genetic imprint of sex is made at the moment of conception, but the formation of a sexual identity must necessarily wait until the time the child is born. Psychosexual differentiation is the outcome of interaction between biological inheritance and social learning, and is the psychological imprint of both sex and gender. The uncertainties surrounding psychosexual differentiation and the lack of hard knowledge as to how and when psychological imprinting of sex and gender take place are at the core of the nature/nurture controversy. Until genetics provides convincing proof to support the position of one side or the other, the problem will not be resolved. In point of fact, one suspects that even that will not still the controversy. The degree to which the biological influences the social, or the sociocultural if you prefer, will likely continue as a matter for conjecture regardless of scientific outcome.

The debate is often emotional, and findings too frequently appear to support the investigator's bias or preconceived position. Any scientific concept can be distorted and misused (Albert, 1966). In all of science there is no such thing as deductive conclusiveness: indeed, according to Goldberg (1973), a scientific theory can never be proved (p. 133). And precisely because theories can never truly be proved, feminists can advance cherished notions—for instance, that the warlike behavior of nations emerges out of the aggressive nature of their (male) leaders—without concern that the notion could be proved false. Intuitively one knows that there is something wrong with statements like "In a society where rigid sex-role differentiation has already outlived its utility, perhaps the androgynous person will come to define a more human standard of psychological health" (Bem, 1974, p. 161), but it is difficult to say exactly what is wrong with it, especially when it is claimed to represent scientific fact. One is reminded of Doob (1935): "It follows . . . that the imparting of knowledge or skill which has reached the scientific stage or of scientific procedures is education and not propaganda" (p. 80).

In recent years there have been a number of research studies proposing that because the real biological differences between males and females are few in number, behavioral differences should also be few. Further, if the number of behavioral differences are not fewer in number, the reason has to be that the sexes are treated unevenly as they are growing up. Their bottom line seems to be that all differences can be explained in terms of environmental influences. The logic is flawed, primarily because the basis of comparison is flawed. These are comparisons drawn between black and white, with unlikes rather than likes. It is well to remember Money and Ehrhardt's (1972) warning: "It is easy to get trapped in circular argument as to whether boys and girls develop different patterns of preferred behavior because they are treated differently, or whether they are treated differently because they demonstrate different behavioral patterns right from the beginning" (p. 117).

## GENDER AND MASCULINITY

Brittan (1989) observes that masculinity and femininity are relational terms. "Masculinity has no meaning in itself—it is always defined in opposition to femininity." Tolson (1977) takes a different approach. According to him,

> masculinity is a culturally specific and socially functional "gender identity" with peculiar (often negative) consequences for men themselves. . . . If gender is cultural and social, then it is also historical. Sexuality is not the same for different generations. There is no "universal" masculinity, but rather a varying masculine experience of each succeeding social epoch. (p. 13)

Thus the question of when and how gender integrates with sex is as historical as it is social and developmental. Sandler, Myerson, and Kinder (1980) have identified four eras of history as having special significance in any study of sexuality. These are (1) the pre-biblical period; (2) pagan-polytheistic cultures; (3) ancient Oriental cultures; and (4) Judeo-Christian influences. They note that of the four the Judeo-Christian tradition has exerted the major influence. The impact of the Judeo-Christian tradition is especially noticeable in the Middle East, Europe, Australia, and the Americas. In this Western tradition, male was clearly favored over female. Other world cultures were also dominated by the male, and the great world religions promoted the institution of patriarchy. The position of man as head of the house with woman subject to her husband was a fundamental tenet of culture and religion. Being male was a circumstance of birth, and religious belief favored him; but becoming a man in terms of gender identity, that is, masculinity, required conscious attention to prescripts and thus was cultural. The preeminence of the male was the status quo of the centuries.

The dominant position of maleness and masculinity was not seriously challenged until the middle of the twentieth century. Although many writers had earlier begun to question whether the system of patriarchy was just, or fair, or whatever, it is generally acknowledged that the work of Margaret Mead (1902–78) was the first to argue that the differences between males and females were marginal and perhaps insignificant. Mead was an anthropologist who traveled the southern seas studying how primitive peoples organized their social systems. In 1955, Mead wrote, "Many, if not all of the personality traits which we have called masculine or feminine are as lightly linked to sex as are the clothing, the manners, and the form of head-dress that a society at a given time assigns to either sex" (p. 190), a conclusion that has been used repeatedly to support the notion that most, if not all, of the differences between male and female result from social learning.

Although in retrospect it is clear that her studies were flawed, Mead's work attracted a great deal of academic attention. It is difficult to understand why Mead could not recognize that the simple behaviors she observed were masking a complexity in social structure, but clearly she did not. Perhaps the natives were telling her what they believed she wanted to know. Without regard to how Mead came to believe, the fact of the matter is that she did come to believe. More important, her observations convinced others to believe. The important consideration is that in the years immediately following the publication of her findings, Mead's notion that differences between men and women had become greatly exaggerated began to be accepted as an article of faith by social scientists. Like many another academic fad, the belief in complete equality between male and female enjoyed great popularity. Indeed, as an article of faith blossomed forth into accepted truth, few scholars questioned either the validity or reliability of cross-cultural generalization. After a number of years, other investigators worked to bring about reevaluation of Mead's work. In the case of Mead's seminal work and the large number of studies that followed her lead, it was clearly a matter of the pendulum swinging too far: biological givens simply cannot be ignored.

With specific reference to gender identity, Masters and Johnson (1974) wrote that "the strength of the sex drive is influenced both by cultural values and by the individual's unique experience of growing up in that culture" (p. 56). Thus, sexuality per se is the actual given: biologically one is born either male or female. The strength of the sexual drive can be assumed to be a biological given as well, in that a healthy person could be expected to have a stronger sex drive than an unhealthy person. Masters and Johnson (1974) were of the opinion that cultural values and the totality of individual experience also impact on the strength of the sex drive, and it would be difficult to find a therapist who would not agree that cultural values and individual experiences contribute to the direction and expression of sexual energy. Weitz (1977) argued that sex role identity is impressed on the child from a multitude of directions, making it impossible to sort out how it comes about. Weitz noted that males and females experience the sexual act in very different ways: "Female sexual identity extends far beyond the sexual act, whereas male sexuality is almost totally encompassed within it" (p. 24). The fact that they experience the sexual act differently means that they also form different perspectives, different meanings. These different perspectives, these different meanings, emerge from the biological given and predispose the individual's set of responses to the cultural, familial, and societal pressures acting to form his/her sexual identity.

The natural process of discriminatory learning occurs throughout the stages of maturational development, and in the normal course of events the boy develops his sexual identity and the girl develops hers. The identities are not identical, but for the most part they are complementary. Yet it is possible to interfere with discriminatory learning—for example, the parent can cross-dress the child—and the results of such interference are highly unpredictable. Because of the unpredictability of affect, interference with discriminatory learning of sexual identity places children at great risk. The boy who will become a man and the girl who will become a woman require equal protection from the theories, the theorists, and any other group of individuals (including parents) who are inclined to experiment with human subjects. The boy is motivated to become a man; the girl is motivated to become a woman.

Theories of human engineering based on androgynous outcome interfere with boys and girls attaining their full adult potential, and would have been dismissed out of hand had they not been enthusiastically endorsed by feminists. Bem (1975, p. 634) provides the particulars: "The women's liberation movement has been arguing that our current system of sex role differentiation has long since outlived its usefulness. . . . Supporters of the movement insist that people should no longer be socialized to conform to outdated standards of masculinity and femininity, but they should be encouraged to be 'androgynous.' " So in fact, the feminist argument seems to be that people should be neither fish nor fowl. But the question arises, who wants that? Whether feminists actually speak for a majority of women is a point worth debating. Consider the following:

It is important to understand that struggles around abortion rights, pro-choice reproductive-rights planks, and lesbianism take place within a political arena that defines woman as mother in the first place. A lack of choice and alternative is necessary to maintain women's primary activity as childbearer *and* rearer. This does not mean that women cannot or do not accept reproductive choice through infanticide, self-induced abortion, the use of contraceptives, and so forth, but ultimately in a society where one's major worth as a woman is judged as a mother, the choice is curtailed. (Eisenstein, 1981, p. 17)

Do these words actually reveal the views of most women? I think not. But even if their views do represent a particular female outlook, it is clear they cannot speak for men. Feminists maintain with some justification that men cannot speak for women. Would not the opposite be true as well? How can women speak for men?

For the individual male, conceptualizations of maleness, manliness, and masculinity transcend personal experience. The way a man experiences his maleness is important, but his assessment of what others believe about him may be even more important. Concepts such as these are strong when one's ego is strong, weak when one's ego is weak.

# 4

# The Significance of Male Bonding

The most sacred and secret of human acts, sex is for closeness and comfort, for reproduction and relaxation, for fun and for pleasure. However, its intimate, delicate, and vulnerable nature makes sex a prime target for physical, psychological, and social problems. Whether innocently or insidiously, sex can easily be sabotaged.

—Sherwin A. Kaufman,
*Sexual Sabotage*

In *A Strange Breed of Cat* (Schoenberg, 1975), the character Mike tells the group that sex is not one of his hang-ups: he might have other problems, but he feels very good about his sexuality. Mike is bisexual, and he is explaining to the all-male group that he never worries about what others might think about his maleness and his masculinity. He believes that he relates well with women because he doesn't have anything to prove, either to them or to himself. The same principle applies when he relates to other men. He doesn't have to act macho with women or play at being tough for guys. Not having to concentrate on jumping into bed with a woman gives him the freedom to relate on other, possibly more sensitive levels with her; not having to worry about whether another guy thinks he's gay gives him the freedom to be himself. In sum, Mike is certain he has his sexual act together.

Mike is lucky, because getting one's sexual act together can be a difficult process. Mike reasoned that he was well adjusted because he was bisexual, and therapists know enough about human behavior to understand the importance that self-perception plays in self-evaluation. In point of fact, the bottom line has to be that Mike was well adjusted because he believed himself to be well adjusted, and (his) bisexuality was mostly incidental to his adjustment. Heterosexual males spend large amounts of time struggling with what they perceive to be homosexual impulses, and Mike's bisexuality removed that kind of concern from him. For the most part, straight males generally manage by happenstance to develop a healthy and positive regard for their sexuality. Gay males are not as fortunate: gay men generally experience the greatest difficulty in building and maintaining positive self-regard.

It is possible to learn a great deal about the harmful effects of aversive social pressure by listening to the personal experiences of gay males. When pressure is exerted to shape individuals into conforming to societal expectations, it is clear that the first casualty is often positive self-regard. Many gays believe that the difficulty many experience in initiating and maintaining lasting relationships is a result of the pressure brought to bear by a largely disapproving society. Support is given to this argument by those gays who report that moving to a large gay community helps them to develop/improve social and interactional skills. Gays have experienced the hate and contempt of the larger society, and many have unconsciously internalized the feelings of this larger society into their own psyche. Again, many report that they were completely unaware that they were internalizing even as they were doing it.

There is a lesson to be learned from the gay experience. Attitudes that others form about you and your persona can be internalized, often to your detriment. It is for precisely this reason that men need to realize that efforts to devalue masculinity pose real and certain risk.

## EARLY INTERACTIVE RELATING

For boys, growing up male is a natural and normal process. Learning masculine behaviors and attitudes is equally a natural and normal process. Further, it is natural and normal for a youth to experience problems in adjustment as he grows to maturity: the road to masculinity is not without obstacle. Stating the obvious, some boys meet with more difficulty than others. Equally obvious, boys and young men do not need the role confusions that feminists, androgynists, and the like have to offer. Gadpaille (1972) writes,

The male is more vulnerable in virtually every way with the exception of physical prowess: there is greater difficulty in achieving maleness and masculinity, coupled with an increased vulnerability of males to disruption of sexual functions and to physical and psychosexual disorders. (p. 44)

The process of adjustment for the very young boy is made easier by the presence of an older male who is available to counsel, to guide, and to teach in both formal and informal ways. The father, be he biological or adoptive, is the preeminent counselor, the preeminent teacher. He teaches moral and disciplinary codes through example rather than through punishment, and explains whenever and whatever his son has difficulty in understanding. Benson (1968) states that

Father serves as an example of how men handle friendships, how they make small talk, how they tell jokes, how they convert light conversation into more serious matters, how they display affection toward women, and so on. He helps his son convert expressiveness into the male mold after it has first been established in experiences with mother and the female idiom. (p. 220)

Older brothers, grandfathers, and other men in the immediate family provide additional instruction, their amount of interaction often depending on how well the father and son are communicating. Later, as the youth moves beyond his family and neighborhood into school and the larger community, his peer group begins to replace father and other family members and in due course becomes the preeminent shaper of his education into masculinity. This is the process by which a boy becomes an adolescent, an adolescent becomes a man.

In a developmental sense, this period can be extremely critical for the boy because he will need help in learning to negotiate the cognitive dissonance that comes about principally as a result of shifting loyalties. The father and other adult males begin to be evaluated in a newer, possibly less favorable light. The prepubescent youth starts to question the wisdom, the authority, even the significance of these older males and oftentimes singles out his own father for special scrutiny. In most cases the wisdom of the father is replaced by the knowledge, perhaps the judgment, of the peer group. This can be a traumatic period in the lad's development, but it is eased significantly when the father or older male is capable of pointing out that distancing is a natural part of the maturing process. If not understood, the distancing can lead to guilt on the part of the son and hurt feelings on the part of the father, or father figure, which will then lead to conflict.

The core issue is independence. To become independent, the boy has to go through a number of successive stages that will successfully challenge the ethical, intellectual, and moral anomalies pervasive in contemporary society. Informal education has to emphasize the affective component of cognition and the cognitive component of affect; that is, thinking has to be tempered by feeling, feeling tempered by thinking. In such a way the boy learns that while the mind must not rule the body, under no circumstances must the body rule the mind.

In an earlier time, an agrarian society nurtured the strong nuclear family that was able to provide the support that a boy needed as he grew to manhood. It might well be argued that in this earlier time role models were more genuine as well because of physical proximity. In addition, the role per se was better defined in that there was general acceptance of the view that conventional adult males were the only really appropriate role model for the male child.

## THE HOME ENVIRONMENT

A male child is born. At a very early age, this male child will begin to imitate and model himself after his father. When neither a biological nor an adoptive father is at hand, the child will attempt to substitute a father figure in the father's role. This adult male can be an uncle, perhaps the mother's live-in boyfriend, but one or the other will make little difference so long as this substitute father treats the child in a loving, caring way. It could be argued that in these early years the actual biological relationship is more important to the adult than to the child. When the father or father figure is absent from the home, primary bonding is delayed.

## BONDING

In a review of Lionel Tiger's *Men in Groups* (1969), Fried (1969) ridiculed the concept of bonding, noting that Tiger's book "shows more resemblance to a political tract than to a work of objective social science," and Weisstein (1976) writes that the work is "an extreme example of . . . maiming and selective truncation of the evidence. . . ." Attacks such as these do more to discredit the writer than the work they are writing about. Perception of course is in the eye of the perceiver, but it might also help to note that using the word "objective" to describe principles of social science is itself a contradiction in terms. In sum, bonding is a useful concept, especially to describe the type of close relationship that can exist between males when there is a purpose for the relationship. Bonding comes about through need, perceived or otherwise. Close friends bond because of shared interests, but other bonding relationships come about because of shared situations. Bonding happens when the individuals involved want it to come about or consciously determine that it will come about. The larger view is that bonding comes about in response to some kind of need. Cox (1976) takes issue with Tiger's claim that males can bond but that females cannot, but perhaps their disagreement is more semantic than real: would it not depend on how one chooses to define the term?

As used here, bonding is defined as a broad concept that describes the process of psychological interaction that leads to gender identity. It is a process that grows out of affiliation in a relationship in which the other person is one judged to be significant. For the boy, the first significant male is his father, or father figure. Later, as the boy's experiential world develops, other males enter into his situation. Teachers, coaches, older boys all become part of the process. Bonding does not always happen, nor is it the invariable outcome of the typical male–male relationship. In fact, bonding occurs only infrequently, but some successful experiences in bonding are developmental essentials. The boy who misses out on bonding relationships, whatever the reason, will experience great difficulty in establishing adult relationships with members of either sex.

Although many factors are at play, bonding is characterized by imitation, modeling, role preference, and propinquity. The amount of interaction matters, and so does the quality. It is important to know that bonding might come about when only one of these factors is in place, and equally important to understand that simple presence of any one or all of the factors is no sign that bonding will take place. At the outset, bonding may be anaclitic, but in time affect generally becomes reciprocal.

## Imitation

The boy growing into adult manhood escapes the grid of environmental determinism by being able to move beyond his experiential self by tapping into the knowledge base that generations of men have bequeathed to him. Viktor Frankl (1966) described self-detachment and self-transcendence as "the nature of human nature" and wrote that these capabilities direct the individual to something other than self; that it, they permit him to expand his experiential horizon. Imitative behavior is behavior that has been copied from some other person; in like manner, one may copy attitudes, ideas, and of course ideals. An actual intent to imitate may or may not be present, and the quality of the imitation appears to depend on the strength of one's ego. In other words, a strong and healthy ego enables the individual to be selective; and being selective means that while behaviors and attitudes can be tried on for size, so to speak, those that do not fit can be effortlessly discarded. The process is a continuing one, stronger at some times than at others. The need or desire to imitate is possibly strongest in early and late childhood, but adolescence brings on a period when it is difficult to separate imitation from role modeling. Although some people do seem to go through life transparently imitating the attitudes and behaviors of others, the overwhelming majority do not. And although the activity cannot be reasonably characterized as being either conscious or unconscious, it is likely that imitation is unconscious as often as it is conscious. The other important thing to know about imitation is that the phenomenon is not always a positive one: Mostly we think of imitation as "aping" behavior, but it can also include "rejecting" behavior. The boy *who does not want to be like his father* is in the same imitative mode as the one who wants to be exactly like his father, the sole difference being that the former is probably not as psychologically healthy as the latter.

When a boy is very young, most parents choose to identify particular behaviors as being "just like" the father. As the child grows, the degree to which the father is imitated also grows. Sex role expectation is an integral part of the developmental core, uppermost in the father's mind for one reason and in the boy's for yet another. There is nothing mysterious about this: the father, or father figure, wants his son to grow up to responsible manhood, and the son wants to be like his father. Positive reinforcement encourages adaptation, with support coming from father, mother, and others in the immediate environment. In like manner, negative reinforcement is used to discourage undesirable or inappropriate imitation. The father's ability to be tender and loving provides the circumambience for the son to express his love and tenderness to the father, and in this setting the boy can learn to imitate the man. The bonding with the father, or father figure, is the child's first relationship of this kind and generally establishes the pattern for any and all bonding relationships that follow.

Men are alleged to be lacking in nurturing behaviors, but a trained observer watching a father interact with his son would question whether this is really so. The perspective provided by history gives clear evidence that the responsibilities attendant on meeting the actual physical needs of his wife and family prevented the average male from taking an active role in early childhood care and development. Until recently, men did not have the time to become significantly involved in their children's lives. Sargent (1977) wrote that men lack the interpersonal skills for intimacy, especially in spontaneity and a "sense of their own emotional life," but this statement is as foolish as it is biased. The situation for men has gotten better, but even today the extent to which a father can become involved in his children's lives may be determined more by economics than by any psychological consideration. It is also true that some men will want to interact with their children more than others, but certainly the same can be said of women.

The newborn has both physical and psychological needs, and in the typical family both parents work to see that both levels of needs are met. Generally, and again when the family and its circumstances are typical, the mother is more intimately involved at the outset in helping the newborn meet its needs. The mother has been carrying the baby within her for nine months or so, and mother and baby have functioned literally as one. Strong physiological and psychological ties are in place. The event of birth does not bring an end to these ties, but physical separation from the mother begins the process of physical distancing that will accelerate until such time as the child is able to function as a relatively independent entity. As the family environment returns to postpartum normality, the father is able to take on a larger share of responsibility for the child's health and welfare. He is able to do this because the logistics are in place; that is, physical separation between mother and child has occurred and family activities are returning to normal. The foundation for the physiological and psychological ties between father and child were also set in place at the time of the child's conception, but strengthening these ties had to await the birth event.

In the first days and weeks of the child's life, interactions and exchanges between parent and child are for the most part parent-initiated. This period of the child's life provides opportunity for the father to get to know his child. In the course of events, as the child grows, the interactions and exchanges become increasingly reciprocal. Imitative behavior becomes part of this exchange, and in time it also becomes reciprocal. But at the outset, as in most other exchanges between parent(s) and child, parents will initiate. They might initiate by starting to imitate some of baby's random activities, such as gurgling. When basic needs are met, baby is happy, and a happy baby gurgles. So, when the happy baby gurgles, the parents will likely begin the process of communication with their offspring by imitating the noises and facial expressions accompanying the gurgling. Baby will have his behavior reinforced by the parents' imitative behavior, and will probably act out an additional sequence of behaviors for the parents to imitate. These behaviors will likely be associated with gurgling, and as they are reinforced, will be added to baby's repertoire. In the beginning stages, the imitative behaviors the parents choose to reinforce and those that baby will copy from parents will be essentially nonselective. For baby, imitative behavior represents the first stage in learning. In the beginning, in this first stage, the objective for reinforcement is to encourage baby to build a repertoire of imitative behaviors. But later, at six months or so, when imitative behaviors become completely natural for the child, reinforcement tends to become gender-appropriate.

Wesley and Wesley (1977) wrote that "psychologists have perhaps overemphasized the concepts of femininity, masculinity, and androgyny . . . giving the impression that these categories involve distinct and deep-rooted personality traits that need to be overcome . . ." (p. 197), and the result is that some parents have indeed tried to overcome. In much the same way that an earlier generation was told that the permissive approach was the only proper way to rear children, with results that in hindsight should have been predictable, parents of this generation are being advised by feminists that making the child aware of his sex might be harmful. Some young parents have been receptive to the advice, and as a result have gone about trying—sometimes with a vengeance—to erase all cues of gender identity from the milieu of their offspring. Such foolishness only proves once again that the ability to sire or bear a child does not correlate with common sense. Besides, in most instances, the larger group impacting on the child will work to provide balance. This group will include siblings and grandparents of course, and aunts, uncles, other kin as well as family friends.

> A great deal of conflict is concentrated in this very small group—all the age-old difficulties of making a family work plus now the conflicting demands of the larger society which calls for all sorts of things that are at odds with the interests of the family and which gives it little honor and encouragement. Still, even in the poorest, most crime-ridden neighborhoods, the youngsters that grow strong are usually those with a strong family behind them. (Johnson, 1986, pp. 123–24)

The child in a nuclear family, deprived of extended family relationships, is more at risk from harebrained schemes in social engineering.

The bottom line in imitative behavior is that behavior that is seen most often will be the behavior most imitated, parent to child and child to parent.

### Imitation Versus Modeling

Psychologists and other mental health professionals are not always careful to distinguish between imitative and modeling behaviors. Both are learning strategies in the same sense that the several types of conditioning are learning strategies, with reward serving to reinforce and punishment working to discourage or extinguish behavior. The principal difference between imitative and modeling behaviors is that the former is incidental and passive while the latter is selective and active. Reward is an important factor in acquisition in both imitation and modeling; but once again it is likely that the way the individual is rewarded is qualitatively different; that is, any reward for imitation is generally extraneous and external to the self, while the exact opposite appears to be true for modeling. Further, differentiation between imitation and modeling is as much a matter of maturation as it is a process of cognitive development; it might be useful to conceptualize imitation as a behavior one generally "grows out of," but qualifying it with the usual disclaimer.

## Modeling

As the male infant grows from infant to toddler, the process of identification with father begins. Selective modeling behaviors begin to substitute for nonselective imitative behaviors, slowly at first but gaining in variety and number as they become positively reinforced. A male child will learn in any number of ways, both verbally and nonverbally, that he shares gender affiliation with his father and not with his mother. A male child will be rewarded by praise, both verbal and nonverbal, when he does model after the father, and this reinforcement will take place whether it is planned or unplanned, wanted or unwanted. A system of rewards will lead to strengthening specific behaviors and acquisition of related ones. Typically, the father will react by teaching the son specific behaviors and actions appropriate for modeling. The son will be reinforced by his father's attention, and the father will be proud of his son's acquisitive ability. Difficult to describe, the interaction between father and son is pleasurable, loving, and rewarding to both. For the child, the relationship with his father is his first bonding with another male. The important consideration is that this is the primary male–male bond and that it establishes a pattern for all the bonds that follow: success in this first bond augurs well for success in male–male relationships; when it does not come about, difficulties can be expected.

The growing bond between father and son seems to have little effect on the relationship between mother and son (Mussen and Rutherford, 1963). There is, of course, no reason why it should, unless one wants to argue that love is finite. As an infant the child has no real way of expressing his love; a cherished belief system holds that a happy baby is one who loves and is loved. But as the infant grows into a toddler and then to a child, he learns how to express love in exactly the same way as he learns to express other emotions. He learns through verbal and nonverbal cues that the amount and degree of affection he receives is often a consequence of his own actions, and in this way his behavior begins to receive parental direction and guidance. Perceptually and relationally he learns to recognize that love is expressed to him in a number of different ways and that he himself is capable and able to express his love in a number of different ways. Incidental to this learning is an appreciation for the qualitative difference between love that is given and love that is received.

Although the child is unable to register these events in any kind of real cognitive sense, this necessarily abbreviated version of the way that he learns to experience love describes how differentiation of emotion begins to take place. When both parents are physically at hand, the infant learns that the way his mother expresses love may be qualitatively different from the way that his father expresses love: both provide comfort and one is not more desirable than the other. But they are different. He learns to value his mother's love and he learns to value his father's love, but gender affiliation/reaffirmation brings on closer identification with the father. Identification is the invariable precursor of modeling, and modeling of father by son is the necessary precursor for primary bonding. In such a casual way, the male child sets into motion the process that will govern the entire spectrum of his behavior for the rest of his life.

### Lessons from the Father

As his son's first real teacher, the importance of the father or father figure must not be underestimated. But of course it has been, and this is one of the principal reasons that adolescent males have such difficulty in growing to adulthood. When a young boy is not able to identify with a strong adult male, it is much more difficult for him to learn values such as personal discipline and personal self-worth. Self-image, or the way one feels about one's self, grows out of values such as a sense of personal control and a feeling of personal control. Because the self-image provides psychological security, the person who does not have a good sense of self is more likely to act out maladaptive and/or asocial behaviors. Benson (1968) noted that "father is not a very impressive figure in American life, and, in slighting him, American social theorists may simply confirm the fact that the behavioral sciences can be influenced by cultural predisposition" (p. 12). In 1976, Green wrote that "father's image has taken a plunge from the craggy dignity of Old Testament patriarchy; today, if he is depicted in a television family comedy, he is usually shown as a buffoon" (p. 132). It may be no coincidence whatsoever that the decline of father as a respected figure has paralleled significant increases in street crime, vandalism, and drug abuse. In point of fact, people use their self-image to order their priorities. Clearly, ordering of priorities is not on the agenda of the infant; on the other hand, the child begins the actual learning of values at an early age. One of the important lessons a father teaches his son is how one goes about ordering his priorities. Both parents contribute to the learning of values in much the same way that they contribute to all learning activities, that is, in unequal measure, with the father contributing more to a son and the mother contributing more to a daughter.

## ADJUSTMENT: THE IMPORTANCE OF DEFINITION

Operational definitions can be a problem in psychology because the way a word or concept is defined can influence the way in which it is understood. The word "adjustment" presents such a problem.

The common thread in any theory of adjustment is the process the individual must go through in order to successfully integrate all the components of personality that the given theorist believes to be basic, or essential. There are a number of theoretical perspectives, but the common thread of any concept is how an individual goes about the task of integrating all components of his personality into one that is completely comfortable for him. A brief consideration of three of these perspectives will provide a background for further discussion.

English and English (1958) assign three definitions to the word "adjustment":

1. A static equilibrium between an organism and its surrounding in which there is no stimulus change evoking a response, no need is unsatisfied, and all the continuative functions of the organism are proceeding normally. (Such complete adjustment is never attained; it is a theoretic end of a continuum of degrees of partial adjustment.)

2. A condition of harmonious relation to the environment wherein one is able to obtain satisfaction for most of one's needs and to meet fairly well the demands, physical and social, put upon one.

3. The process of making the changes needed, in oneself or in one's environment, to attain relative adjustment (p. 13).

Schoenberg and Preston (1983) have noted that an individual can be described as well-adjusted, poorly adjusted, or maladjusted. Their discussion follows.

> The well-adjusted individual, the optimum condition, can be said to have successfully negotiated the internal and external pressures which continuously affect his/her thoughts and behaviors. It can also be said that the individual maintains those internal and external balances which are personally satisfactory.
>
> The internal pressures may be either physical, psychological, or a combination of both. As the name indicates, these pressures arise from within the individual. The physical pressures are those which are physical in origin, e.g., hunger, thirst, exercise. Those which are psychological arise from perceived need, e.g., the need to excel, the need to be accepted, etc. Those which are a combination of the physical as well as the psychological are the psychosomatic pressures, e.g., the need to have sexual relations with a particular person. External pressures are those forces which act on the individual from outside of his own being, e.g., peer pressure, family pressures, etc. As important as external pressures may be, it is important to remember that the individual succumbs to them, for the most part, only when he/she (1) wants to, or (2) does not have reasonable control over the internal ones. When an individual exercises an acceptable level of control over the internal ones, psychosocial and psychopersonal balance is achieved. (p. 154)

Their discussion of psychosocial/psychopersonal balance is as follows.

> Although the number and variety of psychosocial interactions that can influence, alter, or modify behavior are truly infinite, experience tells us that the average individual finds it useful to have behaviors, thoughts, and actions classified into three broad categories labeled (1) family interactions, (2) work interactions, and (3) social interactions. . . . Psychopersonal balance is achieved when an individual is interacting in an harmonious manner with his/her surroundings. . . . Dependency needs cause some people to seek out relationships wherein those needs can be filled: the same can be said for dominance needs, and so forth. Whatever the nature of the relationship, it is neither wrong nor right until and unless the individual determines it to be right or wrong. (p. 156)

Schoenberg and Preston emphasize the importance of interpersonal interaction to their system, which they describe as eclectic and pragmatic. It is an open system, effortlessly coexisting with others. Interactive personality examines the importance of the person and the situation as the preeminent determinant in the formation of personality. Interactive theory provides strong support for the importance of bonding.

The psychoanalytic theory of the self describes the interaction between the id, the ego, and the superego. The main thrust of psychoanalytic theory was set in place by Sigmund Freud, and the theory is neither eclectic nor pragmatic. In fact, one of the more common criticisms of psychoanalytic theory is that its tenets are uncompromising and its practitioners make no effort to accommodate other theoretical positions. The operations of the conscious and particularly the unconscious mind are central concepts in Freudian theory: observable behavior is believed to be a "tip of the iceberg" phenomenon that can be explained only through full understanding of intrapsychic conflict between the primitive wants of the id, the moral consciousness of the superego, and the reality principle of the ego. Kaplan (1965) complained that "many students of human behavior consider the psychoanalytic interpretations of self-development as too mystical and animistic" (p. 127), and his complaint has merit especially when too much time is spent in trying to fathom what is under the iceberg's tip. Most analysts identify the ego as the executive manager that resolves ongoing conflict between the id and the superego, and this specific conceptualization is extremely useful in understanding the importance that a father plays in primary bonding: this first bonding sets in place the base for healthy ego development.

A third theoretical orientation helpful in understanding male bonding is that of Carl Rogers (1951), who was the first to conceptualize personality in terms of the individual's self-concept. Other theorists have followed his lead. In the nondirective system the individual has a view of himself that could be called the ego, but the preferred term is self-concept. But the individual also has a view of himself as he would like to be, which is his ideal self. Although the individual works to maintain the honesty and integrity of his self-concept, he also strives to become the person of his ideal. Personal experience plays its part because we learn (1) from experience, and (2) from how we perceive the way that others see us.

Maslow (1954) described a hierarchy of needs, which he termed as lower needs and higher needs. The earliest needs, termed the lowest, are for physiological comfort. These include satisfaction of physiological needs such as hunger and thirst. The next set of needs, those he termed safety needs, include the need for order, for security, and for stability. Following the safety needs are needs for belongingness and love, and following these are those of esteem (prestige and success). The highest need is that of self-actualization, that is, realization of and satisfaction with self, but others such as knowledge for its own sake and appreciation for the aesthetic can grow out of self-actualization. In a general sense, adjustment is a matter of satisfactorily resolving the needs hierarchy.

## IN SUM

Obviously the child learns from, and interacts with, both mother and father. Physical needs tie the child to the mother for the immediate period after the event of birth, but for reasons that may include affiliation, imitation, and modeling among others, the male child enters into a process of close identification with his father. This process of close identification begins early in the child's life, becoming more pronounced as the infant moves to toddlerhood and early childhood. Father, or father figure, in effect writes instructive messages on the clean slate of the boy's mind, and in such a way helps his son to negotiate the complexities of his psycho-sexual development. The father can help his son internalize capabilities in positive self-control and self-discipline, qualities that will enable him to build a positive concept of self. The bottom line is that it is this positive concept of self that will enable the youth to grow into manhood, certain of his sexuality and equally certain of his masculinity. Both are needed in a world that at times seems to be going mad.

# 5

# Autonomy and Independence

It seems that we fathers hold the key to the violent attempts of the male juvenile delinquent to prove his masculinity and the inability of the male homosexual to achieve masculine identity. Five times as many juvenile delinquents are boys as are girls, and their profile seems invariably to include a weak, absent, or demoralized father. They do hypermasculine things to convince someone, especially themselves, that they are men. Violence is much less likely when there is easy identification with a father figure; compulsive masculinity (which may include heterosexual conquest, profanity, and body building as well as gang violence) appears as an attempted repudiation of natural identification with the mother.

—Eric Mount, Jr.,
*The Feminine Factor*

For the first several years of the boy's life, the primary bond that exists between father and son has the opportunity to grow in love and in strength. The significant others in the immediate environment neither contribute to nor interfere with the forging of this bond. It is likely that part of the boy's affiliation with the father grows out of a conscious distancing from the mother, whom he intuitively comes to recognize as being different from himself and his father. Moreover, long before the child reaches a significant cognitive understanding, his affect tells him not only that he is loved but how that love impacts on him. Internalizing the honest emotions that come from the feeling of being loved enhances his self-worth and will enable him to return the feeling. The reciprocity of the emotion will lead him to intuit that his environment is a safe and loving place, and that the people in his environment are safe and loving people.

## THE IMAGE OF SELF

The first in a series of steps leading to autonomy and independence, a positive self-image is fundamental to the well-being of the individual. This concept of self is largely a social product, and it begins and develops within the security of the family network. One might argue that all members of the family, but especially the mother and the father, interact with the child and thus impact with equal measure. But this is not always true, especially in the case of the male child. Bernard (1975) noted that "parents know the sex of the child from the instant of birth and they lose not a moment in conveying this information to the infant. They fondle boys and girls differently in infancy and are at great pains to deal with them in culturally gender-suitable ways" (p. 47). And Green (1976) wrote,

> Because of father's presence in the family, the whole complicated process known as "father identification" can take place. . . . It is difficult to say just what the term means, [but] it seems to come down to a child appreciating the existence of a significant adult, wanting to be like him, being willing to learn from him and wanting to be accepted by him as significant in turn. (p. 70)

Appropriate gender behaviors are reinforced by a father who wants his infant to grow up as a "real boy" and by the mother who is pleased to see her son grow up in her husband's image. It comes down to this: a complex system of rewards and punishments is set in place to reward those behaviors that are gender-appropriate and earn disapproval for those that are gender-inappropriate. To note that little boys are given teddy bears and masculine toys while little girls get dolls and feminine toys echoes the usual banality, but on the other hand this particular cliché does happen to be true. Moreover, we should be grateful that it does continue to be true because gender differentiation is not the unimportant issue that feminists and androgynists have made it out to be. As Brenton (1966) has written, "It's difficult to conceive of a boy who is given a girl's name, consistently dressed in girl's clothing, and encouraged to play with dolls and such growing into a man at ease with his own sexuality. Many psychiatrists can point to cases of male patients who have had childhood patterns similar to the one I have just outlined; these patients are possessed of an enormous fund of personality problems" (p. 68).

## GENERALIZATION OF SOCIAL LEARNING

As the male infant grows to toddlerhood, then to early childhood, his patterns of learning generalize to incorporate a growing and expanding number of social and personal interactions. The ability to socialize in this larger milieu has been determined in large measure by earlier social encounters with the parents and with members of his nuclear and/or expanded family. The young child will meet with difficulty when he interacts with his first set of playmates, simply because he is met with the formidable task of adapting a set of skills into a completely new situation. However, if he has the strong sense of self that allows for values determination, skills generalization should happen in a relatively brief period of time. A parent can anticipate that the child will meet with some initial difficulty owing to the fact that the ability to generalize from one situation to another is a skill one learns with time and with practice. But initial difficulty must not be confused with persistent difficulty, and the difference between the two should be keenly understood.

Key elements of concern are (1) the kind of problems the child is meeting with, and (2) the degree of difficulty he is having in negotiating resolution. For example, the kind of problem could possibly be that he is either not getting his way with his peers or is not receiving from them any explanation as to why he is not getting his way. This type of problem is common and often requires nothing more than the intervention of a significant adult who can explain the dynamics of the situation to the child, in terms he is able to understand. Social interaction, regardless of age, is a matter of experiential learning. The child who has experienced a good level of social interaction in his home is far ahead of the child who has not been so fortunate.

If the primary bond with the father has been set firmly in place, and if the child feels comfortable in his relationship with his mother and with other family members, he will be ready to enter into a chum or sidekick relationship with one of his neighborhood friends. The interaction usually develops because of propinquity, that is, they live close to each other and are provided with opportunity for spending time together. These relationships are important, and often a great amount of time is needed before the friendship is cemented. Once in place, these relationships tend to be strong. What is important about the chum or sidekick relationship is that it provides the first opportunity for peer bonding.

This early stage of childhood development is spent in testing and eventually validating attitudes and behaviors already learned. It is in fact a matter of testing out in the field the lessons one has learned in the laboratory. When the lessons one has learned in the home are productive in the play area, the rewards the child receives are both intrinsic and extrinsic. They are intrinsic because the child feels good about himself, and they are extrinsic because others feel good about him and tell him that they do. The reward system contributes to an ongoing building of a strong ego, or the healthy concept of self that is called self-esteem.

From a developmental perspective, it is unlikely that much conscious thought is given to matters of sex or gender prior to the formation of the first and then subsequent peer relationships. With a father or father figure in place, it is likely the boy will have internalized a level of personal identification that affirms for him (1) that he is a boy, and (2) that there is reward when he acts and behaves as a boy. Interacting with his peer group in general and with his buddy in particular initiates a new process, a growing consciousness of the special significance of sex and gender. And, once again, it is a matter of testing attitudes and behaviors in the laboratory before using them in the field.

As the boy gains experience through a widening network of social exchanges, he begins to develop confidence in his ability to use the skills previously learned in the milieu of the family. As his level of confidence grows, he becomes more competent in learning to deal with a marginally different reality-set from that to which he had previously been exposed.

As one example of the kind of situation he must confront in this new reality, consider the change that will inevitably come about in his conceptual framework of his perceived self, that is, his perception of how others regard him. In the immediate past, the boy did not have to question whether the significant others in his life valued him: he was confident of the love and understanding of his parents and all others who entered into his family setting. However, he soon learns that his playmates are not always supportive of him. He senses that arguing with his playmates carries a completely different set of risks from those growing out of arguments with his parents. He may indeed have argued with brothers and sisters, possibly cousins, prior to arguments on the playground, but a referee in the form of an adult family member seemed always at hand to mediate differences. Increase in the degree of freedom carries with it a reduction in the amount of direct supervision, and as a result the boy and his friends are more able to confront one another. For the first time in his life the lad may begin to hear phrases like "I don't like you" or "You're not nice," and these negative comments have the potential to be disruptive to his sense of perceived-self. Family members generally do not threaten physical violence, nor were they likely to cause him to have the feelings of separation anxiety implicit in the "I'm going to go home" argument when events did not go their way. Direct as well as implied threats add a new dimension to his perception of self, and reactions formed at this stage of life are critical determinants of later response patterns.

With this as a given, it is easy to understand why learning how to play is one of the most critical developmental tasks of early boyhood. Discrepancies between how he perceives himself, how he is perceived by his family, and how he is perceived by his playmates are not easy for a child to resolve. But resolve them he must, and in order to do so he must have the guidance and support of his family.

## LESSONS FROM THE PLAYGROUND

The playground is the child's first laboratory.

In many science courses, a student fails the whole course if he does not do satisfactory work in the lab. Fortunately, the boy who fails Playground 101 is not going to fail life. On the other hand, the boy who experiences difficulty on the playground will likely carry the emotional scars into adulthood. There is an urgent need for a boy to be successful in interacting with playmates at this early stage of life, which is the compelling reason for parents and other members of the child's family to monitor playground experiences. The ability of the child to integrate his play activity into those of his peers can be rated as an emotional and behavioral bellwether. If the child experiences continuing difficulty in playground relationships, the parent should try to determine if the problem is of the child's own making or if it is somehow beyond his control. This requires an objectivity that can put a severe test to the love a parent has for his child: taking the child's part is by far the easier course of action. Whatever the transaction, it is essential that it be explained to the child so that he can learn from the experience. Children are no different from adults: they will press forward even when they know they are wrong. Consider the message that the child receives when he knows he is in the wrong, but has his parent's support. It is clear that the child will learn either that he will have his parent's support no matter what he does, or that it's incredibly easy to deceive one's parents. Neither of these is a worthwhile message: the one causes the child to be spoiled, the other teaches him to be arrogant.

### The Playground Bully

The obvious statement to be made about bullies is that they come in all shapes and sizes. It is never easy to deal with them, and a cardinal principle seems to be that ignoring them does not work. As well, observation of children at play bears out a truism that most of us learn through experience, that is, that "giving in" to a bully brings on increased jeering. The lesson seems to be that a bully must be confronted as soon as possible, at an appropriate time and place. It is not easy for any child, especially a sensitive one, to act assertively in a situation charged with hostility. Moreover, there is no best way to deal with a bully. The child must understand that there are options other than fight or flight. The lesson is most effective when it is learned as part of early playground experience.

The playground bully generally does not have a strategy. What he does have is a range of tactics that he has found useful in helping him get his way. These may range from emotional blackmail to physical force, and all points in between. The child who says he won't play (or won't let others play) unless one thing or another happens is using emotional blackmail, a tactic possibly more difficult to deal with than the threat of force. Children used to having their own way at home are going to want to have their own way on the playground: They will see nothing wrong in the way they are behaving because their global view of their world, which of course is not global at all, places their wants and their needs at the center of the universe. They have not been taught to interact on a level that is best termed "sharing," and as a result really do not know better. It is not uncommon for a child to appear to be bullying when actually he is not, the explanation being that he simply has not learned the appropriate social skills.

In situations such as these, the children need to be given a reasonable amount of time to resolve their issues. When they appear unable to do so, adult intervention explaining the "rules" of play will usually be all that is needed. But when maladaptive behavior continues, stronger measures will have to be taken because bullying behavior rarely goes away unless it is directly confronted. No one wins from such behavior: the bully will be emboldened by his success, and his victim will incorporate his loss into diminished self-esteem. The behavior cannot be ignored, because in all likelihood the bully will simply escalate his demands, and "giving in" will also result in more of the same. Helping a child face up to a playground bully is not pleasant, and if nothing else works, the child might have to be emboldened to go through the painful experience of standing up to his tormentor.

## DISCIPLINE, FREEDOM, AND RESPONSIBILITY

Social skills learned on the playground complement and refine those learned earlier in the home environment, and in turn will be refined and complemented by those to be learned in school. It is sobering to realize that the social skills the child learns from home, playground, and school are those that will determine in large measure the success he will have in life. Considered within this context, the need for parental supervision and guidance becomes obvious. It is equally important to understand that the supervision and the guidance that are clearly necessary at this early stage of development have to be carefully balanced against the child's increasing need for freedom and autonomy. A central principle in child rearing is that parents need to exert virtually one hundred percent responsibility at the beginning of the child's life and marginally reduce this percentage every day that the child lives. In such a way the child learns to take responsibility for himself. There are no guidelines, no hard-and-fast rules as to how the activity is to proceed. On the other hand, there is much evidence to suggest that the process must be conceptualized in maturational terms. Further, problems of a serious nature can best be understood when the process is linked to maturation.

Piaget, reported by Rosen (1977), distinguished between heteronomous morality and autonomous morality, the former describing the law of others and the latter subject to one's own law. Applied in a general sense to the child-rearing process, the law of others, that is, parents, teachers, and so on, governs until such time as one's own law initiates self-governance. The process is as inevitable as it is complex. In other words, the individual is going to progress through the several stages of development to the point where he takes control of his life *whether or not* he has received the appropriate level of education, training, or experience. In like manner, the individual will learn (or fail to learn) to exercise traits such as self-discipline and personal control. It is absolutely certain that the child who does not learn, at home, that personal freedom carries with it a full measure of responsibility will be completely irresponsible in the way he exercises his personal freedom: he will not respect the rights of others because he has never been taught respect for himself. Just as heteronomous discipline describes the discipline imposed externally and autonomous discipline describes that degree of personal discipline that we impose upon ourselves, so heteronomous freedom is that freedom we are given, autonomous that which we allow ourselves, and in like manner, heteronomous responsibility is that which is controlled by others and autonomous that which we exercise in our own interest. The common thread to discipline, freedom, and responsibility is the way they are learned, that is, imposition prior to internalization. The boy who is not taught these qualities has mostly his father to blame, because the primary bond is the enabling element.

## SOCIAL SKILLS

The acquisition of social skills is listed as one of the principal developmental tasks in early childhood, but for the boy the acquisition of gender-appropriate social skills is the essential task. For the most part, the task is not a difficult one. Imitative and modeling behaviors are the initial learning strategies, and neither of these requires any significant degree of conscious attention. Taking the learning out of the playground/laboratory into a wider experiential field, the boy begins to play with other boys. Some of these may be older, but for the most part his playmates will approximate his own age. He will learn to regard his group of playmates, and especially the older boys, as role models worthy of his imitation. These newer models do not replace the emotional bond that the boy has with his father. In fact, it is likely the boy will be successful in accepting the new role model *because* the primary bond is in place. Apportioning of affect can be a painful process if the boy worries unduly that he is distancing himself from his father. The dissonance leads to conflict, the precursor of guilt. Rewards, punishments, and other reinforcing strategies provoke a measure of reflection about behaviors per se, a level of acquisition that is appropriately termed reinforcement learning. Most important, reinforcement learning is the forerunner to the formal and informal instruction strategies and is therefore an indicator of the success an individual will meet with in developing his intellect. In other words, difficulty with the informal strategy of reinforcement learning suggests additional difficulty with the more formal learning strategies.

The bond that the boy has forged with his biological or adoptive father is the foundation for personal relationships. A strong primary bond augurs well for success in initiating and maintaining all personal relationships to follow, and the reverse generally is true as well. But a question arises: If the primary bond is of such great importance, what are the implications for the boy who is reared in a home in which the father is absent? Every indication suggests that it is easier for everyone involved when a loving, caring father is influential in the child's development. Loving and caring are key descriptives: when these qualities are absent, for whatever reason, the void has to be filled by someone else. Single mothers can fill the void with the help of a boyfriend, uncle, or grandparent.

Social skills are taught in response to both felt and perceived needs; that is, the child feels, the parents perceive. Readiness, as a concept, describes whether the learning is appropriate for the given developmental level. Generally, informal instruction, that is, "talking about it," paves the way for the more formal instruction that is to follow. From this perspective, it becomes clear that informal instruction can be used to provoke thought, suggest need, or anticipate readiness. When the child is inquisitive, the expedient use of informal instruction contributes to readiness. The reverse may be true as well: the child who shows no interest in learning may become frustrated or even hostile if pressed.

When the child is ready, but learning is delayed because instruction is either unavailable or not forthcoming, the child will do the best with what he has. What this means is that he will be forced to make decisions on the basis of inadequate, inappropriate, or simply misleading information that may or may not serve his interests. In the short term, on the level of playground interactions, the problem may not be very serious: the lad may have difficulty with his friends, he may be a bully or even a loner, but he will survive. No one dies from improper sandbox play; still the traumas associated with painful early childhood experiences are as real as they are inevitable. The long-term result can prove to be quite destructive in terms of any number of possible outcomes. The bully who has not learned how not to be one will press on with his bullying, the loner will not suddenly learn how not to be alone, and the mind forced into making rash judgments can in time become comfortable with the belief that it is not necessary to have the facts before the decision is made.

There are strong links between the biological, the social, the psychological, and the behavioral. The child on the playground has many concerns, many issues, which for the most part arise from attempts to integrate the sum of these parts into the whole. Some theorists refer to this "whole" as personal identity; others term it self-concept, or ego. Personality will develop into a whole whether the parts are integrated or not, the difference being that successful integration is a good predictor of adequate personality function.

This early stage of development is characterized by efforts the child makes to distance himself from his parents, particularly his mother. Komarovsky (1976) has written, "Independence from parents and the ability to assume responsibility for one's own life is a central component of the masculine role in our society. The manifest goal in the socialization of male children is to ensure their emotional and economic emancipation from the parental family" (p. 198). If the father–son relationship has been good, that is, bonding has taken place, the distance the boy wants from his father amounts to a kind of emotional independence. The boy is developing new friends on the playground, and he has some concern that these new friendships will affect the relationship he has with his dad. He may not be able to put his feelings into words, and he worries. As he tells his father about his new friends, he studies the reaction. When the reaction is perceived as supportive, the process is affirmed. Should the father not be seen as supportive, the boy will press on with the new friends but perhaps with less confidence.

Fromm (1956) described mother's love as indulgent and unconditional, father's as conditional. This distinction would seem to suggest that the process of distancing would be more hurtful, causing more problems for the father than for the mother. However, this does not appear to be the case, and the explanation possibly arises out of Fromm's belief that father's love has to be earned whereas mother's love has no strings attached. The love the mother has for her son may be more simple and more natural, but for the son the distancing process from his mother is more involved, more complex, and has the larger potential for causing problems. This suggests that a mother's love may be more simple and natural, that it is freer, and that it is given without condition. The fact that it is given without having to be earned may explain why the boy experiences greater feelings of guilt dissociating himself from his mother than from his father. "Earning" love is not the same as "receiving" love; "I don't want to have to earn it" does not carry the emotional impact of "I don't want to have it given to me."

Thus the distancing process from his mother is far more complex, posing a set of problems very different from those that arise in distancing himself from his father. Distancing brings about problems for the mother as well. Lynn (1964) noted that "demands for typical sex-role behavior come at an earlier age for boys than for girls . . . at an age when boys are least able to understand them . . . in the absence of readily available male models" (p. 19). The son has been comforted by his close relationship with his mother. Again, he cannot be expected to give words to his feelings, but distancing himself from his mother both physically and psychologically brings on feelings of guilt. Perhaps it is only on an intuitive level, but the boy does recognize that in order to behave more like his buddies he must begin to think less like his mother. He lacks understanding of the dynamics of his situation and has little or no appreciation for ways his behaviors and attitudes have to change, but becoming friends with the playground peer group is pleasurable activity and is personal affirmation that he is "growing up." These are the guidelines; if distancing himself from his mother is the price he has to pay, there is no doubt that he will pay it. He will be conflicted because his developing needs for independence and autonomy seem to be denying the important role she has played in his life. Moreover, he may well worry that she will withhold her love if he moves away from her. A great deal depends on how the mother adapts to the developing situation: the mother who is able to become reconciled to the fact that her "baby" is growing up and no longer needs her to the extent that he once did will ease the boy's burden. The child will become increasingly resentful of the mother who is not ready to let go, and the mother–child relationship will suffer.

## LESSONS LEARNED IN AND OUT OF SCHOOL

Jersild (1960) noted that the child's development may be healthy or unhealthy depending on the state of health of the society in which he lives. "A state of health prevails when the influence in society combined with the impetus of a child's own growth help him to realize his potentialities; an unhealthy situation prevails when a child's development is distorted by forces in a society which impose stifling stereotypes" (p. 15).

For uncounted numbers of children, attending public school is proving to be an extremely hazardous experience. Sometimes the learning situation is unhealthy because the school is a reflection of the unhealthy social community surrounding it, but more often the learning situation is unhealthy because an unchallenging curriculum breeds apathy and stifles creativity. For children above the level of dull normal, school is usually a boring place. It is boring in the lower grades and it is boring in the upper grades. A few students continue to receive excellent education within the public school system, but one suspects they do it in spite of rather than because of the system. The awful reality is that the average student can move from grade to grade without doing much in the way of work and will graduate from high school if he doesn't become too much of a discipline problem.

The influences of the home, the peer group, and the school are the principal shapers of the child's character and personality development. The process is as sequential as it is ongoing: that which is learned in the home is expanded by knowledge gained from the peer group, and the process is continued as the child moves through the lockstep grades of the school system. The child attempts to integrate as he matures, and one measure of his maturity is the success he has in doing this. Another measure of maturity is the degree to which he is able (1) to personalize, and (2) to become comfortable with the totality of his changing reality. Erikson (1959) stated that "the growing child must, at every step, derive a vitalizing sense of reality from the awareness that his individual way of mastering experience is a successful variant of the way other people around him master experience and recognize such mastery" (p. 89). Unless the parents are lazy and/or hopeless, the child will be stimulated by his interaction with them; with their encouragement he will form affiliations within a peer group that will also challenge him with new and varied stimulation, both cognitive and affective. The school situation is quite another matter.

There is a general perception that schools are going from bad to worse. The situation does not appear to be as desperate in elementary grades as in middle or secondary school, but this is about the only positive comment one can make about the education available to the overwhelming majority of children. Parents are made to feel that the problems associated with some schools have neither beginning nor end, and there is a sense that teachers and administrators share the foreboding. The problems confronting the public school system are complex and many. What the child learns or does not learn in classroom and schoolyard are incredibly consequential in the development scheme of things. The fact of the matter is that students are being shortchanged by an educational system in which the curriculum has been weakened and discipline has almost disappeared. Erikson's (1959) "vitalizing sense of reality" has been replaced by the depressing reality of a few students running amok while the rest of the students (and their teachers) search out ways to defend themselves. Discipline is often nonexistent. The bottom line is that a growing number of schools, particularly in large metropolitan areas, are simply not healthy for our children.

The critical issue is the mixed message that the school experience provides in essential developmental areas such as (1) self-discipline; (2) personal awareness; (3) motivation; and (4) personal control. The process of child development is sequential (Schoenberg and Preston, 1983). The child matures, his world expands, and an increasing number of people begin to enter into the world of his personal experience.

## THE ORGANIZATION AND MANAGEMENT OF AUTONOMY

The period of adolescence marks the time when the young male takes his longest strides toward autonomy. When he successfully negotiates the hurdles, he becomes independent. The vernacular expression for independence is "becoming one's own man."

Autonomy is simply another word for independence. The autonomous male is a man who self-regulates, one who is able to think as well as act for himself. It is a fact that freedom to act is generally circumscribed by forces external to self, which tends to suggest that no one is ever complete autonomous. Thus, becoming autonomous means exercising independence to the degree that one has decided is the optimum for him. How to achieve optimum independence? The building blocks are, again, (1) self-discipline; (2) personal awareness; (3) motivation; and (4) personal control. Each will be discussed in a later chapter, but it is necessary to mention them here because each is essential to the growth, development, and management of autonomy, each makes its unique contribution to the total personality. Schoenberg and Preston (1983) have argued that

> within the generalized structure of universal concepts there are highly discriminative specific applications to each unique situation. For example, a person might intuitively recognize that by appearing even-dispositioned to her peers, she will meet with greater acceptance. However, long periods of experience with her parents might have reinforced the view that sullenness or even confrontative behavior is a more certain method of getting what she wants. So, the difference is really one of discrimination. (pp. 65–66)

Clearly this discrimination within the generalized structure explains how the individual is able to alter or transform persona. In one way this is good, but in another way it is not. It is good when it enables the individual to be flexible: the persona becomes the role, and the role adapts to the situation or circumstance. A less than positive dimension is that continued success in adaptive role-play might make it easier for the individual to switch personas as the need arises, and suggest that it is quite all right to be different things to different people. Understanding this phenomenon helps to explain problem behavior, but in a larger sense this phenomenon is the term of reference we use to rationalize behavioral shifts that may or may not be out of character. For example, parents often continue to see their son in a very favorable light when practically all others who come in contact with him can label him quite the contrary. Knowing how easy it is to adapt one's persona and the role one wants to play in differing situations should convince even the most permissive parent of the need to carefully monitor the many directions in which their son is moving, and to evaluate the many new friends the son is making.

Carefully monitoring does not mean complete control or total supervision. Quite the contrary. What it does mean is showing their son that their care and concern is ongoing even though he is growing away from them, that they understand the process of development that he is going through, and that they intend to be supportive and helpful to the limits of their ability. They must ensure that their supervision is recognized as supportive, that essentially it is nonthreatening. Difficulties can arise when parents are not careful to explain their reasons for ongoing monitoring, the end result usually being that the teen-ager becomes resentful because he believes that their concern indicates a lack of trust or worse, that they want to continue to exercise control over him. Murphy (1960) suggests that "the parent will supply restraints primarily when the child is defeating his own ends, especially when the child is showing, as most children do sooner or later, that he actually wants goals, order, and a sense of direction rather than chaos. But it will be his first concern that the child live in the child's own idiom before he be asked to understand the idiom of others" (p. 317).

The adolescent is not a child of course, but neither is he an adult. Especially in his early teens, a boy feels the stress of being positioned between childhood and manhood. Virginia Woolf asked, "What could be more charming than a boy before he has begun to cultivate his intellect? He is beautiful to look at; he gives himself no airs; he understands the meaning of art and literature instinctively; he goes about enjoying his life and making other people enjoy theirs." It has also been observed that no one ever really grows up because no one really ever wants to grow up, an observation especially appropriate for teen-age boys. Adolescents have their feet planted in two camps; mostly the positions are compatible, but the point to be emphasized is that they are not completely compatible. The boy's role is a complex one; he can be helped along by his parents, but mostly he has to do it himself.

His parents should be guided by the boy's interests, and should be prepared to give him rein as he requires it and slack as he requires that. Fathers in particular should attempt to recall the way they felt when subject to parental supervision, and perhaps allow experiences to suggest how best to deal with their sons. But they must also recognize that their sons, to say nothing of the times, are quite different, and this suggests that their approach may have to be modified to fit a different reality. However, *plus ça change, plus c'est la même chose.*

# 6

# In Search of Self

Do what thy manhood bids thee to do, from none but self expect applause;
he noblest lives and noblest dies who makes and keeps
his self-made laws.
All other life is living Death, a world where none
but Phantoms dwell,
a breath, a wind, a sound, a voice, a tinkling of the
camel-bell.

—Sir Richard Burton,
translated from *The Kasidah of Haji Abdu Elyezdi*

According to Bednarik (1970), "the abrogation of the male role is making itself felt in three distinct areas: the erotic, the sphere of male activism and aggressiveness, and finally the sphere of male authority.... The male crisis does not originate in the sexual sphere; it erupts there, being caused by general social conditions governing relations between the sexes and by disturbances in areas other than that of sex" (pp. 122, 47). Not everyone would agree that the male is in crisis. For instance, feminists are not apt to agree because their world view centers on women's issues. Other one-issue groups might be expected to be guided by the same level of logic. Still, taking quick stock of the problems besetting the world as well as the complex problems that seem to surround us, it seems incredibly unlikely that there is no relation whatsoever between the male in crisis and the world in crisis. Feminists have argued that the chaos is the end result of having men in control, but people generally have not been persuaded that this is actually the case. There is logic to the argument that men are more responsible for the mess the world is in, but clearly this is simply a matter of numbers: more men than women have been elected to positions of power. The fact is that only a relatively small number of women have achieved positions of power, but even though their numbers have been few in comparison, some of them have proved that women are also capable of dreadful leadership. Several have done so with great style, great panache.

The rules have changed, and that's part of the problem. Yet it is also true that the new rules are frequently biased in favor of women, leaving men confused as well as angry. The Supreme Court of the United States has disallowed the right of free association. In the matter of Rotary International for example, the Court removed the club's right to determine eligibility for membership. It is interesting to note that the Supreme Court of Canada has displayed a greater sense of responsibility: this body of justices has ruled that such matters are not appropriately dealt with in the courts. Sometimes the foolishness goes further. Amiel (1984) reported on one judgment of the Canadian Human Rights Commission: "Sexual harassment that does not otherwise adversely affect the woman's employment may nonetheless be discrimination on the basis of sex if it simply makes the work environment unpleasant." Amiel noted that "if the tribunal's judgement is taken literally, it means that if an employer, by a glance or a remark, acknowledges the gender of a female employee and she does not like it, we have sexual harassment."

Reverse discrimination appears to mirror the ethical and institutional breakdown that is so disruptive to North American society. Writing in *Time* magazine, Bowen (1987) observes that "large sections of the nation's ethical roofing have been sagging badly, from the White House to churches, schools, industries, medical centers, law firms and stock-brokerages—pressing down on the institutions and enterprises that make up the body and blood of America." One section of Bowen's article is particularly interesting.

Surveying the damage, Church Historian Martin Marty of the University of Chicago sees a "widespread sense of moral disarray." Once, notes Bryn Mawr Political Scientist Stephen Salkever, "there *was* a traditional language of public discourse, based partly on biblical sources and partly on republican sources." But that language, says Salkever, has fallen into disuse, leaving American society with no moral lingua franca. Agrees Jesuit Father Joseph O'Hare, President of Fordham University: "We've had a traditional set of standards that have been challenged and found wanting or no longer fashionable. Now there don't seem to be any moral landmarks at all." (p. 28)

A learned friend once referred to the American involvement in Vietnam as a classic example of "self-righteousness gone berserk." The point he was making was that a group of prosperous people on one side of the ocean had taken it upon themselves to make important decisions for a group of not-so-prosperous people on the other side of that ocean. In this case it was a matter of one group deciding that since democracy had worked so well for them, it would work equally well for the people of Vietnam. The people of Vietnam were not listening: they hungered for rice more than they hungered for freedom, proving once again that the hierarchy of needs works on the national level fairly much as it does on the individual. Freeman (1976) wrote that "the warlike attitude which goes along with an idealization of physical strength and dominance is proving to be positively destructive" (p. 149). Vietnam was not the first time a military power used its strength to promote a national agenda, and it is unlikely it will be the last.

## THE ADOLESCENT MALE IN CRISIS

When Bednarik (1970) formulated his views on the male in crisis, it is likely he was troubled by the ease with which cherished notions can be promoted as theory. In the first instance, what is reasonable in theory is not always feasible in practice. It is, after all, reasonable to believe that all people want the freedoms that go hand in hand with democracy; it is not realistic to believe that a desire to be free transcends the need to be fed. In like manner, it is reasonable to believe that it is wrong to indoctrinate young males into a completely rigid system of masculine values; it is not realistic to believe that the way to avoid indoctrination is to teach them no masculine value system at all. The adolescent male is in a crisis of his own, brought on by the reality of his changing world and his changing body. Mead (1967) has written that

the chief trap for the boy in this pattern of maturation lies in the conditional nature of the whole process. On the one hand, he can always win applause by taking the next step, moving from the third team to the second team, from the position of the worst in his class to the position of next to worst, by gaining a pound or growing an inch; the applause is hearty. . . . On the other hand, none of this acceptance or applause is final. If the next step is not taken, then the approval becomes only a remembered happiness, now withdrawn, which must be worked for again. (p. 311)

In my view it is the parent's responsibility to ensure that the process is not conditional. The adolescent meets with new as well as revised physiological, sociological, and psychological circumstances on a daily basis that are changing him as well as discomfiting him. The boy may be well on his way to becoming an adult male, but in the process he will have to sort out the complexities in establishing and maintaining a growing number of male and female relationships. The ease with which he makes new male friends has been determined in large measure by the strength of the primary bond, and from these new friends he may find one or several boys with whom he will bond. At this stage of development, making friends with girls can be more difficult than making friends with boys. Fullerton (1977) writes, "An important part of socialization in adolescence is learning how to perceive and interact with persons of the opposite sex, to be intimate with someone who is different. The childhood experience was one of intimacy with someone similar to the self, someone with whom the child could identify" (p. 188). Adolescence is the period of a youth's life when he dreams about what kind of a man he will be and the kind of work he will do. According to Levinson and his associates (1978),

A man is supposed to get out there and do something: perform, accomplish, produce, bring home the bacon. If his body is a vehicle for demonstrating his masculinity, he tries to acquire special strength, endurance, sexual virility, athletic prowess. If his mind is the preferred vehicle, he uses thought as a weapon in the struggle to win, to outmuscle his rivals, be it in science, art, or chess. Whatever the arena, he want to establish his place in the world of work and men. He wants to become a productive, independent, responsible, authoritative man who has the mental and bodily capacities needed to attain his goals." (p. 233)

The adolescent is not sophisticated and does not contemplate his future in terms such as these, so part of the continuing role of the father consists in helping his son construct an agenda he is capable of attaining.

## SCHOOL AND THE MALE SOCIETY

It appears that the majority of boys do better with their studies in elementary school than in either middle or high school. The curriculum is said to be irrelevant; but it's worthwhile to ask the question, irrelevant to what? An elementary or middle school is the place where a student should learn the principles of learning. He should learn to read and to write, to be sure, but he should also learn how to study as well as memorize. In other words, students have to be taught to learn. Elementary school in particular should stress the principles of learning; secondary school should refine these skills. Trades and business schools, colleges and universities are the centers of learning in which specialization occurs. The matter of what to teach is simple enough: in the early years, the basics; in middle and high school, expansion beyond the basics; in postsecondary education, specialization.

One of the large problems with contemporary education is that it has been shaped too much by a social engineering agenda. As a result, students are not challenged by a rigorous curriculum. There has also been such a breakdown in discipline that the matter transcends the issue of providing the tranquil milieu that is essential to learning: an extraordinarily large number of students are at physical risk every day they attend classes. Another significant issue is that of feminization. A number of investigators have discussed the issue. Sexton (1969) writes,

> Though run at the top by men, schools are essentially feminine institutions, from nursery through graduate school. In the school, women set the standards for adult behavior, and many favor students, male and female, who most conform to their own behavior norms— polite, clean, obedient, neat and nice ones. While there is nothing wrong with this code, for those who like it, it does not give boys (or girls either) much room to flex their muscles—physical or intellectual. (p. 29)

The same point of view is expressed by Stoll (1973), who argues that the problem with the feminized school is that "if the boy absorbs school values, he may become feminized himself. If he resists, he is pushed toward school failure and rebellion" (p. 65). Fullerton (1977) argues that "the boy raised in a predominantly female world, where his mother and female teachers are the primary adult models, finds it difficult to define masculinity ... the boy raised primarily by women tends to define masculinity through a negative process: he is to be nonfeminine.... Lacking positive models for masculinity, he has to invent his own images of manhood" (p. 181).

The inventive mind of the typical adolescent male will have little difficulty in forming images of what a "real man" is all about, but whether his conceptualizations are real or not is an entirely different matter. The degree to which inventive roles affect behavior continues to be debated, but a large number of social scientists do express concern that immature viewers run a serious risk of getting a blurred view of reality from watching the characters on television soaps, dramas, and such. But to be sure, there are the wider implications. For example, if we should be concerned that adolescents (and other immature individuals) are at risk from viewing inappropriate role models on television, should we not also have great concern about inappropriate role models in the adolescent's life situation? In fact, we probably should have *more* concern: viewing television is passive learning, whereas sitting in a classroom *should* be active. There is little doubt that male students are at risk.

## THE THEORETICAL STRUCTURE OF PERSONALITY

In considering the sex- or gender-specific structure of personality, it should be obvious that theories of personality are generally not addressed to either sex or gender. The intent of a theory is to explain the origin or evolution of a general principle, and quite often the explanation is made in terms that are as broad as they are general. There are exceptions, for some behavioral, attitudinal, and/or emotional characteristics of personality are in fact more appropriate to the study of one sex or one gender, but for the most part the principles describe members of both sexes and both genders.

Hilgard (1962) offers as good a definition of personality as any. "The term *personality* is used to mean the configuration of individual characteristics and ways of behaving which determines an individual's unique adjustment to his environment. We stress particularly those personal traits that affect the individual's getting along with other people and with himself. Hence personality includes any characteristics that are important to the individual's personal adjustment, in his maintenance of self-respect" (p. 447).

Cochran (1978a) argued that personality can be most appropriately understood as a relational concept rather than as an entity. The individual defines his/her personality in terms of encounters with other people, and most especially those with friends and significant others.

English and English (1958) summarize the definition of personality as follows: "In ancient Rome the *persona* was a theatrical mask, whence came the notion of *appearance*, of the individual as socially perceived. A second sense was that of *role*, the part played in the drama. A third meaning was that of the *player* himself. Thus, the *personality* came to mean the outward appearance (even the false appearance), and also the true inner being or self" (p. 382).

Interactive Personality Theory (Schoenberg and Preston, 1983) is relational in that the individual defines himself in terms of his skill in interacting with all those with whom he comes into contact, most particularly his friends and significant others. Personality characteristics develop slowly and in a manner that mostly resembles trial-and-error behavior. According to these theorists, the individual develops the ability to interact successfully as a result of successful experience in interacting: there is no other way. The child is taught, the adolescent puts what was taught into practice, and the adult refines the learning through the process of continuing interaction. The principal characteristics to be learned are (1) self-discipline; (2) personal awareness; (3) motivation; and (4) personal control, which this approach suggests as four components critical to development. In the Interactive Theory of Personality, these characteristics are believed to be essential to the development of personality, to personality integration, and in maintaining the psychological and emotional balance that enables personality equilibrium. It is clear that the eventual mastering of these characteristics is as much a matter of learning as it is training and/or indoctrination. They are important because, once they have been learned, the individual is able to recognize them as useful guidelines.

On a marginally different level, the several theoretical approaches that grow out of a defined concept of self give strong emphasis to the attitudes the individual employs to monitor his interaction with his universe. He will think in these terms and will do so without regard to whether or not he wants to think of himself in this way. Throughout his life he will evaluate himself in terms of who he is, who he wants to be, and what others think about him.

In these systems, these several perspectives form the self (the ego), the ideal self (the ego ideal), and the perceived-self. The perspective that emerges out of self-appraisal is the self; what the individual wants to be is the ideal self; and how he believes others have come to regard him forms the basis for perceived-self. In the literature of psychoanalysis, the processes and activities of the mind are termed the psyche. Ego, when used in the psychoanalytic sense, refers to that aspect of the psyche that is conscious and most in touch with reality. This is a somewhat different use of the word, and can lead to confusion. But the confusion will never be serious, first, because the meanings are not altogether dissimilar and, second, because when the word "ego" is used in *psychoanalytic* reference, it is usually used in conjunction with the id and the superego. These other two aspects of the psyche represent the unconscious, which is "a collective name for unconscious psychic activities" (English and English, 1958, p. 569), and the superego, which attempts to impose conscience. Self-esteem grows out of self-awareness, which itself is constructed on (1) a strong concept of self; (2) appropriate distance between the ego (or self) and the ego ideal (the ideal self); and (3) reasonable satisfaction with his notion of how significant others have come to perceive him. In the final analysis, the way personality is structured in any theoretical sense is not as important as how the individual comes to view his own unique personality structure. Besides, the differences in theoretical structure are not necessarily exclusive; that is, it is not antitheoretical to refer to a person's ego ideal and the degree to which he is motivated all in the same sentence.

An interactional theory of personality integrates three basic dimensions: (1) recognition that how he presents himself to others is in part a self-definition; (2) understanding the variety and complexity of the roles he will be expected to fulfill; and (3) maintenance of personal continuity across situations and in the face of both internal needs and external pressures. But as Schoenberg and Preston (1983) have pointed out, the integration of these dimensions will continue to be tentative because the individual has to maintain homeostasis.

## SELF-DEFINITION

If we truly want to know how a man defines himself, we must study his style of interacting. Obviously we must ask with whom he interacts, but answers to other questions might be even more informative. For instance, are the quality interactions at home, with friends, or in the office setting? If these are either at home or in the office, does this mean that he interacts best when he is operating from a position of power and/or influence? The answer to "when" should shed light on the importance the man places on relationships, and "why" and "how" as follow-up questions should help us fill in the blanks.

### Self-Discipline

Among the characteristics of personality essential to a strong, masculine definition of self, the degree to which a man is able to discipline himself is the first among equals. If the individual is undisciplined, the odds are that he will not be able to motivate himself, or be in control of himself, or have a good sense of his own personal dynamics. The boy who learns discipline from his parents at home and from his teachers in school is indeed fortunate. Sooner or later every individual has to learn a certain amount of self-discipline. Schoenberg and Preston (1983) state that "a general rule of thumb is that the later in life one learns and begins to practice self-discipline, the more difficult it is to learn" (p. 68).

Self-discipline cannot be taught in the traditional sense, nor can one be instructed in motivation or personal control. The groundwork is laid in the home by parents who themselves are keenly aware of the difference between discipline and punishment and are able to successfully communicate this distinction to their son. Disciplining a child is essential for healthy growth. It takes time because the reason for its use has to be explained to the child. The child has to be taught to experience discipline as a process as normal to his growth as either eating or drinking. Punishment is a different matter: it is reactive, and generally does not require explanation beyond linkage. To be sure, it is sometimes difficult to sort out the difference between discipline and punishment. The result has been that people opposed to punishment will say they are opposed to discipline as well. But discipline is instructive, punishment corrective. Once the distinction is learned, benefits accrue. This does not mean that the boy invariably agrees with disciplinary measures, and it is by no means a simple task to convince him that discipline is in his long-term interest. But both can be done, and both should be done so as to defuse residual resentment. The important consideration is that at the outset discipline is enforced from the outside, by an outside authority. In due course, if the discipline has been seen to be fair, the lad will internalize those elements of discipline that he has come to accept as adding value to his well-being.

### Personal Awareness

The most obvious aspect of personal awareness is sensitization to the people, the events, and the cause/effect relation of social stimuli. Unlike self-confidence, personal awareness can be taught using traditional teaching methods. The individual who is gifted with average intelligence can learn the importance of a personal agenda, and appropriate ways to communicate this agenda to other people, while demonstrating a concern for the sensitivity and the needs of significant others. Deficiency in personal awareness skills suggests one of two probabilities: (1) the individual was not taught the skills; or (2) he resisted learning them. Since pressure from a nonconforming peer group is the usual reason underlying resistance, parents are provided with another very good reason for closely monitoring their children's friends and associates.

## Motivation

The subject of motivation has been one of continuing interest to psychologists and other social scientists. People are motivated to behave, or behave in a certain way; people are also able to motivate others to behave, or behave in a certain way. English and English (1958) list need and goal as anchors for the concept: need refers to deficiency and goal to objective. The rewards for motivated behavior are internal (intrinsic) as well as external (extrinsic), and it is likely that the rewards for the person who motivates are the same. There is no evidence that intrinsic motivation is the forerunner of extrinsic motivation, but it seems likely that the one would lead to the other. There is the suggestion that if one is somehow coerced into the performance of a task, success will reinforce the actual performance and engender additional interest in performing. Maslow (1955) suggested that the concept of motivation should be most appropriately considered as being differentiated into *deficiency motivation* and *growth motivation*. He defined the former as motivation to fill a need and the latter as an essential component to self-actualization. In their discussion, Hutt, Isaacson, and Blum (1966) have suggested that "growth motivation is closely related to the development of conscience and ego-ideal, since it has to do with the development and maintenance of distant goals." Finally, Schoenberg and Preston (1983) have stated that becoming motivated is a highly individualized phenomenon, and that the person can be motivated "against" as well as "toward."

## Personal Control

In their discussion, Schoenberg and Preston (1983) suggest that it is often difficult to distinguish between the characteristics of personal control and self-discipline. They write, "Control, like discipline, is an outgrowth of parental guidance and instruction. Both attributes share an intellectual component in that: (1) a certain amount of intelligence is required to negotiate the shift from external to the internal; (2) judgments are required to determine the appropriate reaction to each and every situation; and (3) the maintenance of systems which are in one's best interest requires a high level of subjective objectivity" (pp. 69–70). One distinction that can be made is that personal control is more closely related to the attitudinal, while discipline is more closely related to the behavioral, but forcing discrimination between the two characteristics is in the final analysis not at all necessary. Schoenberg and Preston (1983) conclude that "training . . . begins early; or rather, should begin early. The parents—and other significant others—relax external controls as they perceive the maturing child internalising what—for them—are appropriate personal control mechanisms" (p. 71).

## THE ORGANIZATION OF THE SELF

The self is organized around a balanced perspective, which in sum is more than education, training, and/or experience. The boy begins his search for self with the sense of identity that has been provided to him by his parents, teachers, and friends. He adds his own set of personal experiences to this sense of self, factoring in his perceptions of the judgments of significant others. His belief system emerges out of what he has been taught, what he has observed, and what he has experienced. When his behavior and attitudes conform to his belief system, that is, his personal code of ethics, he is a typical adolescent, mostly well adjusted but having peaks and valleys on his road to responsible adulthood.

Friedenberg (1959) has said that "adolescence is the period during which a young person learns who he is, and what he really feels. It is the time during which he differentiates himself from his culture, though on the culture's terms. It is the age at which, by becoming a person in his own right, he becomes capable of deeply felt relationships to other individuals clearly perceived as such" (p. 29). But the time frame of adolescence spans at least seven years, in a calendar sense; in a developmental sense, it may take an even greater length of time for an adolescent to get his physiological, psychological, and social act together. Individual differences, and primarily those in the areas of intelligence and physiological development, are critical factors in determining the rate at which he will progress to become a person in his own right; or in the vernacular, his own man. Differences in mental and physical development set the adolescent apart from his peers; sometimes the difference works in favor of the adolescent, sometimes it doesn't. If the boy is bigger and stronger than other boys his age, he may be able to use his size to his advantage; if he is intellectually superior to his peers, that superiority could work to his disadvantage if he is not careful how he uses his intellect. Individual differences also appear in skills and common-sense knowledge, in attitudes and in achievements, and in all areas where competency is a factor. And it is not only the difference that matters: how the individual feels about the difference and how he perceives others feel about his difference may be even more important. The fact is, growing up is a very difficult job.

The intimate links between the biological, behavioral, and the social ensure filtered generalization of strengths and weaknesses throughout all dimensions of personality. Successful experience tends to promote successful experience; unfortunately the reverse seems to be true as well. It becomes clear then that a primary responsibility for parents is to provide experiences in which the adolescent will be successful, without regard to venue. Adolescents will encounter situations where they fail, perhaps miserably. Parents commit gross error when they try to completely discount either the failure or the situation; what they should be providing is the perspective in which the failure should be seen. Telling a disheartened adolescent that "experience is the best teacher" or that "we learn from our mistakes" does not provide the kind or level of support that he needs, nor does it address the real issue of cause and effect or probable consequence. At least one equal part of the failure equation is the question "What now?" The question, asked or unasked, must be answered to the adolescent's satisfaction.

Adolescence is a time of crisis for the adolescent. For the caring parent, adolescence seems to be *a time of one crisis after another*. Each crisis must be managed; when the adolescent can handle the crises on his own, so much the better. In this way he will learn crisis management, which is simply another description for learning to manage his own affairs, or becoming his own man. His developing personality reflects a personal identity that is in transition from boy to man, a complicated process that includes internalizing characteristics such as personal control and self-discipline while defining in his own terms and for his own needs the several appropriate concepts of self. There is much else to learn, but the adolescent will be able to ease into a mastery of what he needs to know if the basics are in place. His is not an easy job, because adolescence is a difficult period. But like the actual act of breathing, the process is as natural as it is normal. Like breathing, the way it is actually done is difficult and tedious to describe. Finally, and again like breathing, the activity carries with it its own momentum, which is as constant as it is ongoing. Evans and Potter (1970) have written that Merton's notion of a *self-fulfilling* prophecy might suggest that "adolescents possibly would not experience an identity crisis if only they were not told by society that it was expected of them" (p. 66).

# 7

# Interaction: Integration of Learning and Subjective Experience

> In interpreting social behavior we are confronted with a spiraloform model. James anticipates what John will do. James also anticipates what John thinks he, James, will do. James further anticipates what John thinks he expects John will do. In addition, James anticipates what John thinks James expects John to predict what James will do.
>
> —George A. Kelly,
> *The Psychology of Personal Constructs*

The relationship between identification and identity is not always spelled out as clearly as it should be. The words are sometimes used as if they were synonymous or interchangeable, but they are neither. In a significant way, identification is the precursor to identity. Establishing one's identity means processing every bit of formal and informal learning through a filter of subjective experience, made subjective because identification with the attitudes and behaviors of others has provided the pattern. Identity defines the person. In addition, identity provides the parameters of social behavior, which by definition is the way we want to present ourselves to other people. Thus, if identity can be conceptualized as defining the way an individual has come to think about himself, social behavior gives form and structure to those attitudes we have come to believe are worthy of display to all with whom we associate.

A man's search for his unique personal identity is never completed, because the concept of self is fluid and will continue to change as his reality changes. The male infant grows into the boy, the boy grows into the man, and each step of the way means facing and somehow resolving issues related to identity and self-concept. "Facing" does not mean confronting, nor should "resolving" be understood as reaching a satisfying solution. "Facing" could mean withdrawal, and "resolving" could also mean walking away from the issue. Stress can result whether the issue is faced (or not faced) or resolved (or not resolved).

People experience stress on three separate and distinct behavioral levels: the physical, the social, and the psychological. Growing up male provides many opportunities for stress on *each* of these levels.

## THE ROLE OF STRESS IN THE INTEGRATION OF LEARNING

English and English (1958) have defined stress "as a force, applied to a *system*, sufficient to cause strain or distortion in the system, *or*, when very great, to alter it into a new form" (p. 529). Within the context of this text, it is important to view stress as a failure to make appropriate and satisfactory adjustment in the three significant areas of the person's environment, that is, his family life, his school or business life, and his social life. And as previously noted, stress is experienced on three separate and distinct behavioral levels. These several perspectives provide a broad understanding of the dynamics of stress: the cause/effect relationship plus the relationships likely to give rise to it. Stress is generally manifested in fear and/or anxiety and is the principal contributor to psychosomatic disorder. The verbal equivalent of fear/anxiety is worry, and the nonverbal language accompanying it is very often a literal wringing of the hands. The effects of stress on personality range from the mildly debilitating to the completely disruptive. Clearly, the manner in which an individual learns to cope with stress has tremendous implication for the quality of his life, and his life style. This fact is sobering, but understanding that stress can play a significant role in the way we learn may be an even more alarming dimension.

Many men report that they did not learn to play sports in adolescence because of fear of being perceived as awkward or uncoordinated. However, sports are not the only activities that men do not become involved in because of the fear of looking inept. Consider the simple activity of dating. Teachers and counselors become aware of the private agony endured by a significant number of male adolescents who do not date because they fear rejection. It is tempting to bolster the morale of young men so afflicted by telling them that rejection is part of growing up and that they must not let the fear immobilize them, but such advice might deepen the hurt. Like everyone else, adolescents resent being told that their hurts are not important.

The adolescent must be helped to effectively deal with feelings such as these. Helping him deal with the hurt is the immediate goal; the secondary one is working to minimize long-term effect.

## ATTITUDES, BELIEFS, AND OPINIONS

In 1966, Katz wrote that "attitude is the predisposition of the individual to evaluate some symbol or object or aspect of his world in a favorable or unfavorable manner. Opinion is the verbal expression of an attitude, but attitudes can also be expressed in nonverbal behavior" (p. 55). The English and English (1958) definition of "attitude" provides greater detail: attitude is "an enduring, *learned predisposition to behave in a consistent way* [italics added] toward a given class of objects ... not as they are but as they are conceived to be" (p. 50). In his discussion of beliefs, attitudes, and opinions, Kendler (1963) observed that "man, who finds himself in many different situations, is motivated to maintain a consistent set of beliefs throughout them all. *This tendency to remain consistent is one of the major factors controlling the crystallization of beliefs, attitudes, and opinions*" (italics added) (p. 595). From the foregoing it seems clear that an attitude once formed is an attitude that will remain, sufficient reason for parents to be concerned with the attitudes taking shape in the intellect of their sons.

Attitudes can also be a source of great stress for the adolescent. A well-known explanation of the phenomenon of cognitive conflict is the theory of cognitive dissonance (Festinger, 1957). According to this theory, a person experiences cognitive dissonance when one of his attitudes, such as honesty, is inconsistent with another of his attitudes, such as cribbing on an exam. The individual experiences conflict as a result of dissonance, the degree of conflict generally correlated with the significance of the issues. Dissonance is resolved when internal consistency is restored. It is also true that some can learn to live, even thrive, on ambiguity. It is reasonable to conclude that anyone who consistently breaks legal, moral or ethical codes has in one way or another resolved his issue of being able to live with dissonance through the artful technique of marginalizing the behavioral code. Using the example of honesty versus cribbing, attitude consistency can be restored by either rejecting cribbing out of hand or somehow convincing oneself to believe that cribbing is acceptable behavior.

While rejecting dishonest behavior is clearly the more appropriate alternative, for the adolescent it may not be the more reasonable. If the value has been clearly taught by word and by example within the home, the probability is that it will win out over the alternate value; but it may involve the adolescent in quite a bit of soul-searching before he does decide to uphold his value. And of course there is the possibility that he will not stay with the value: the adolescent could opt for the other alternative, especially if it is easier or appears to be more rewarding. "Everyone is doing it" and "I'll do it just this once!" are appealing rationalizations, and it is in struggles such as these that the adolescent is able to profit most from parental guidance.

### Attitude Development

An increase in the amount of social mobility has brought about an almost revolutionary change in people's attitudes. People are mobile to an extent unimaginable mere decades ago: they move from their own neighborhood, their own city, in order to sample the events of the larger world that surrounds them. Public automobiles and public transportation provide physical mobility, allowing people to work and play in relatively distant locations. Cinema and television afford a kind of mobility as well. The visual media expand the awareness of the viewer beyond that of personal experience. Radio was different; people listened, but the degree to which people attended was (and is) qualitatively different. Prior to television, the formation of attitudes took place within the home, school, or peer environment. Now the situation has changed: the number of influences is limitless.

An argument could be mustered that television promotes self-indulgence in society, but a counterargument is that television simply reflects a self-indulgent society. The truth lies somewhere in between. We live in a self-indulgent society, and it is likely that a viewer will unconsciously adopt many of the attitudes, beliefs, and opinions that he sees on the television screen. Most parents give up on monitoring what is being watched once the child grows into adolescence, but this is a mistake because monitoring should be continued beyond childhood. The answer to the question "When does monitoring stop?" is purely and simply "When there is no longer a need." Parents should be able to make that judgment. Personal control has to be set firmly in place.

Helping an adolescent develop reasoned, sensible attitudes is largely a matter of ensuring that he is provided with the kind of information that will allow him to construct his opinion. In his childhood years the attitudes a child internalizes tend to be those of parents, teachers, and friends. The parent who believes that his son is learning the wrong kinds of attitudes is usually able to make environmental adjustments, that is, move the boy to a different school or encourage him to make other friends. In adolescence the attitudes the teen-ager adopts as his own are more likely to be those of his friends and of the constructs he has picked up from television and the movies. The impact of parents and teachers is lessened, and it is not quite so easy to encourage the adolescent boy to make new friends. His mobility allows him to have whomever he wants as friends. The problems associated with motion pictures and television pose even more difficulty for monitoring, but that does not mean it cannot be done. Internalized conscience and attitude/behavior control come from the outside, and the system should have been set in place long before adolescence.

When the system either has not been set in place or not satisfactorily, the parent might on occasion have to adopt a heavy-handed approach. It might indeed mean that a parent could be forced into telling his son something akin to "As long as you live under my roof you will do what I tell you to do." And mean it! If the relationship between parent and son is good, the ultimatum will be used infrequently, if at all. As well, it would be reserved for issues of great importance. The point is, parents should not overuse the tactic but neither should they be afraid to use it when circumstances require. In this same context, the father or mother should be aware of the implied threat contained within the message and must be prepared to follow through with the threat—if that is what it takes. Despite what they say, adolescent males want direction. On the other hand, they are not stupid. If a teen thinks he can have his own way, he will press for it. If he is able to bully his parents, he will do so. He will lose respect for them in direct proportion to the success he has in getting around them.

### Attitude Formation as an Expression of Self-Esteem

It seems likely that people with high self-esteem form healthier attitudes than those with low self-esteem. It would also seem likely that parents who themselves have positive attitudes toward self are in a better position to help their children develop the positive attitudes that ensure a high level of self-esteem. On the other hand, there is no certainty that this will happen; many youngsters seem to be eclipsed by their parents, whatever the reason. Nor should parents believe they have to accept total responsibility for their children's self-esteem, whether high or low. Friends, acquaintances, and teachers may play an even greater role. It is truly impossible to predict or explain where one learns his attitudes. The same can be said for attitude formation.

Adolescents build on, possibly refine, the notions and opinions and beliefs to which they were exposed as children. When these notions, opinions, and beliefs become fixed, they are then referred to as attitudes. In the final analysis, unless the person is afflicted by a learning problem that renders him incapable of separating right from wrong, the individual himself determines what he thinks, as well as what he does not think; what he believes, as well as what he does not believe. Attitude and cognition are complementary as well as reciprocal; that is, each person builds a framework of thinking that reflects his attitudes, and at some point his attitudes begin to influence his thinking.

Children's attitudes are formed in a straightforward way: parents teach by word or example. In adolescence, the formation of attitudes becomes much more complex. Some adolescents will continue to be governed by the attitudes of their parents, but for many teens growing up means growing apart. Throughout this developmental period, parental responsibility requires an ongoing monitoring that should be unobtrusive but must not be without consequence. Attitudes reflect the essence as well as the style of the persona, and are critical factors in development. In that sense attitudes shape the individual, not only who he is but as well who he can become. Generally, attitudes are most healthy when they fall somewhere in the middle of a continuum. On the one hand, they must be subject to change; on the other, they should not be changed without cause. Attitudes are shortcuts to closure and understanding, so in effect they influence cognition as well as behavior. In fact, exaggerated expectations grow out of ill-formed attitudes. In *A Strange Breed of Cat*, the psychologist-convenor noted that "we preconceive experiences and situations, and when we learn that our preconceptions are not an accurate reflection of the experience or situation, we become disillusioned. And maybe the disillusionment isn't a resultant of anything other than disappointment with the preconception, per se, rather than with the situation or experience" (Schoenberg, 1975, p. 94). When attitudes are shaped by expectation, they become subject to the anticipatory type of error brought on by lack of information or misinformation growing out of spiraloform judgment. Finally, in a discussion intended to emphasize the importance of attitudes and attitude formation, it is appropriate to note that Frankl (1977) termed attitude "the last of the human freedoms—to choose one's attitude in any given set of circumstances, to choose one's own way" (p. 104).

## Aggression and Attitudinal Set

Psychologists have spent a great deal of time studying aggression, and most investigators have concluded that the behavior is learned rather than transmitted through genetic imprint. Scott (1958) provided something of a qualifier when he noted that "the actual observed behavior of people in our society is consistent with the biological facts observed in the great majority of other mammals . . . that males tend to be more aggressive than females . . . it cannot be argued that biological factors have no effect . . ." (p. 87). Hutt (1972) is more specific: "Any scientist interested in developmental processes, when confronted with such a consistent sex-dependent behavioral phenomenon which prevails despite changes in time and space, and which is shared by other species of some phytogenetic affinity, is constrained to examine the biological origins of such a phenomenon" (p. 109).

Still, those who do argue the biological side of the argument will concede the effect of "intellectual override," that is, that learned behavior rather than the reality of a differentiated organism is the larger factor in determining the individual's level of aggressiveness. Still, if there is consensus that aggressive behavior is a product of learning, it has to be noted that no such consensus exists vis-à-vis how the word is defined or what the concept is supposed to mean. It is important to understand this for the very simple reason that because different people have different ideas of what constitutes aggressive behavior, the conclusions that investigators reach will have validity only in terms of their respective definition. This means that whatever is said or written about aggression, and most certainly about aggressive behavior, will reflect the author's bias.

In his discussion of aggression, Goldberg (1976) noted that "from early boyhood on everyone expects the male to be aggressive. The expression of it is, however, expected to be nonpersonal, directed against strangers, competitors, enemies, and other outside targets. At home or in school the boy's aggression is severely curtailed. He is not allowed to fight back, to lose his temper, to be boisterous, to insult, to confront, or to fight" (p. 61). But is aggression a simple matter of being boisterous or losing one's temper? Some authorities would agree. In their definition, English and English (1958) state that aggression is a "hostile action . . . which causes fear or flight in another animal" (p. 19). Lewin (1935) termed the adolescent "a marginal man" having goals and objectives that his culture will not allow him to reach. He handles the resulting frustration in one of two ways: either he becomes aggressive or he somehow withdraws from the field.

A more explicit explanation is given by Goldenson (1970) in *The*

*Encyclopedia of Human Behavior*: aggression is "violent, destructive behavior usually directed toward bringing suffering or death to other people, but sometimes displaced to objects or turned inward to self" (p. 44). One problem with this definition is that aggression is not always violent or destructive; there is also verbal aggression. Obviously a shouting match could lead to fisticuffs, but more likely it will lead to some level of stand-off. Aggression, like hostility, can be displaced; it can also be manifested by withdrawal, either from the scene or from the situation. But the second and more serious problem with this definition is the implication that aggression is bad, which leads logically to the understanding that the aggressor (and aggressive behavior) is also bad. It may be a case of what you see is what you get. In other words, some aggression is harmful; as a behavior it can be counterproductive for the user and hurtful for the person to whom it is directed. Other aggressive behavior is not harmful: the user can attain his objective and other persons can be encouraged to compete. This view coincides with that of Bednarik (1970): "In principle the possibility of aggressive behavior is inherent in all active and voluntary behavior. Conversely it follows that active behavior of any kind harbors a germ of aggression, that every kind of activism contains an aggressive element. . . . Only our subjective evaluation of our own or other people's activism brands it as aggressive or non-aggressive" (p. 159). The old saying "Your right to express yourself ends once you enter into my airspace" can be appropriately applied to aggression.

In sum, there is nothing inherently wrong with aggressive behavior. To argue that aggression can get out of hand and that the aggressor can get out of control states the obvious. The point worth making is that each and every behavior in a person's repertoire can be counterproductive or hurtful when exaggerated, or acted out to excess.


## MALENESS, MANLINESS, AND MASCULINITY

Fullerton (1977) wrote that "the quest for identity is often self-defeating, because what more people search for is a label, rather than a living, developing person. It is this sense of identity as a detachable 'thing' that is the crux of alienation from self" (p. 45). This notion of looking for the labels is a very real problem for many adult men, partly because most were led to believe in stereotypical conceptualizations of maleness and masculinity but also because parents have not done enough to aid their sons in developing introspective skills. From an early age boys are encouraged to make their own decisions and to be self-reliant. The adult world signals a number of expectations to them, but the message is not always clear.

Sometimes the message is clear but the signals are mixed. As one example, the message may be that of honesty but the signal is "don't get caught." Decision-making is learned within a developmental sequence, a process not unlike that of learning to exercise personal self-control.

Perhaps the most important contribution that parents, and especially fathers, make to their sons is helping them to develop the cognitive and affective frames of reference that will enable them to internalize the traits and characteristics of responsible manhood. There is so much to be done, so many lessons to give. It is certain that every youth will develop a cognitive as well as an affective frame of reference. It is also certain that every individual will internalize these frames of reference into an experiential repertoire that will give meaning and direction to his life.

There has been a great deal written about maleness, manhood, and masculinity: some of it good, a lot of it bad. At times the emphasis has been on labeling the man rather than the man himself. In point of fact, it is difficult for a boy to grow into a man. There are many developmental tasks to master, and an extraordinary amount of material to be learned. The boy adapts, or the boy does not adapt. Then the man emerges from the boy. The man adapts, the man does not adapt. When coping skills are keenly honed, the credit has to be shared between the boy who learned and the man who had the wisdom to refine. When they are not, the blame must also be shared, by the boy who did not learn and the man who did not recognize the deficit.

The man who is confident of his manhood and proud of his masculinity owes his confidence and his pride to the boy who preceded him. It is really quite that simple. No matter what is said, no matter what is written, the boy who has been responsibly looked after will have the strengths needed to endure the tests put to him. And no matter what is said, no matter what is written, the man who emerges from that boy will also have the strengths needed to endure the tests put to him. Some will argue that this is a remarkably simplistic protocol for such a complex phenomenon, and to an extent they are right. However, developmental progress is characterized by increasing differentiation and increasing integration. The progress is not necessarily steady: more likely it will be made in fits and starts. Inconsistent discipline is worse than no discipline at all, and punishment that cannot be enforced must never be threatened. The point is, raising a boy to manhood is remarkably simple provided ingredients such as love and responsible caring are in place.

But what of the disciplined youth who matures into the delinquent adolescent? Or the male, whether young or old, who becomes so harassed by situational issues as to be literally transformed into a person quite at odds with what he might have been before? In actual fact, examples such as these are the separate issues they might appear to be. Conceptual functioning can be disrupted by trauma or insignificant event alike; and who can successfully argue that interruption did not grow out of flawed concepts rather than trauma or insignificant event?

## The Characteristics of Masculinity

The characteristics of masculinity have been argued and discussed in great detail in the literature of psychology and the social sciences, but even the most cursory reading underscores the differences in opinion. It seems clear that masculinity and femininity are not the bipolar opposites they were once believed to be, but dissimilarities abound. The reason for the differences are for the most part environmental and grow out of experiential differences. Smith (1968) noted that "differences between men and women never apply to all men and women, never are self-explanatory, never are constant from one group of men and women to other groups, and never establish the superiority of masculine or feminine characteristics" (p. 458). What then are the characteristics of masculinity? When people talk or write about the characteristics of masculinity, what do they mean? And what characteristics do they include?

The ideals of manhood and gentlemanly behavior suggest a number of characteristics that men by tradition are encouraged to internalize into their own personal codes. Honesty and integrity give strength to character and therefore are considered to be essential gentlemanly traits. A singularly important characteristic is that of behavioral directness: exemplified in motion pictures by the straight-talking, straight-shooting cowboy. A gentleman by definition has an abiding belief in justice and fair play; he tends to be calm rather than emotional, empirical rather than rational. He can be both gentle and sensitive, especially to women and children, but aggression channeled into a keen competitive spirit tends to mask these softer characteristics in his interaction with other men. The masculine man is rough and he can be tough, but most of all he has successfully disciplined his mind and his body to a keen edge. These are the ideal goals, and it is clear that many fall far short of the ideal. Still, it is probably safe to speculate that most men do try to achieve goals similar to these. As characteristics of one gender, they are neither superior nor inferior to those of the other: despite psychobabble, men and women get on best when their roles are complementary.

It is likely that the adult male who has problems adjusting to a masculine persona was unsuccessful in attempts to bond with other males. Although a number of descriptives are applied to the man who seems to be at odds with either his maleness or masculinity, the term "wimp" is really hard to beat. As it is used in the contemporary vernacular, the word describes a male who is weak and indecisive. The word is probably shorthand for wimple, a cloth formerly worn by nuns to cover the neck. Since the qualities of behavior associated with a "sister" are the polar opposite of those expected of an adult male, the word accurately describes a "weak sister," that is, a man who has not learned to think and act in ways appropriate to his gender. In short, a "weak, insipid male *person*."

A wimp has the biological and physiological givens, but lacks the emotional/psychological characteristics of mature masculinity. Possibly the problem is one of identity, growing out of a faulty father–son relationship. The boy deprived of this primary bond will meet with difficulty in subsequent bonding efforts owing to the lack of a first experience in an atmosphere of trust, caring, and warmth. In a developmental sense, emotional and physical growth is sequential; when for one reason or another the growth is impeded, short-circuiting takes place and growth is inhibited. When an adult male perceives that he is different from other adult males, the usual result is loss in self-esteem and compensatory destabilization in the form of the fight-or-flight syndrome. It may very well be that withdrawal is the most common reaction to any perceived inadequacy; one has to suspect that hostile behavior is a close second. In other words, although wimpish behavior is usually perceived as passive-avoidance, it is sometimes masked as passive-aggressive or confrontational acting-out behavior. Stansby (1972) might refer to wimpish behavior as outer-directed, that is, behavior controlled by external events, a construct describing "those individuals who lack the stabilizing direction of a well-integrated self and a coherent self concept" who "tend to display different characteristics with different groups of people . . ." (p. 51).

In any event, if the word "wimp" did not exist, it would have to be coined to describe those adult males who seem to have never quite mastered the art of manly or masculine behavior. Wimpish behavior is not necessarily related to physical strength, but it could be; or to intellectual ability, but it could be; or even emotional stability, but again it could be. It could be a function of the one or possibly all three at once.

# 8

# Psychosexual Adjustment

The stereotyped male as a woman-conquering sex machine is not the proper description of the majority of American men. Most men, like women, are sensitive, romantic, caring . . . and fearful. And it precisely these qualities that make them vulnerable to numerous sexual problems.
—Sherwin A. Kaufman,
*Sexual Sabotage*

At any developmental level, the number and quality of peer relationships are key elements in the way the individual comes to terms with his sexuality. The interacting the boy does with his mates prepares him for the more complex interactions of adolescence, which are in turn refined and enable the man in due course to become intimately involved with another human being. In the same way that primary bonding sets the pattern for all male relationships that follow, the interactive skills the boy learns from childhood friendships become transferred to adolescent dating experiences and establish a lifelong pattern for emotional and physical relating.

In psychosexual development, these stages represent the essential learning experiences. In childhood, and for whatever reason, the boy who is unable to form close friendships with other boys will have difficulty moving on to the wider circle of adolescent interactions that will include girls. Obviously the boy will have had friends who just happen to be girls long before he enters adolescence, but the way he evaluates their friendship undergoes dramatic change as he himself undergoes the dramatic changes of puberty. Finally, the adolescent's experience with dating will provide the general framework for the way he learns to relate with women in general, and one woman in particular.

The tasks to be met in each of these development stages are fairly specific. The principal ones are (1) establishing and maintaining peer relationships; (2) earning recognition; (3) integration of experience; and (4) management of physical and intellectual growth. The developmental timetable is an individual matter, but like the organization of the self represents a mixture of attitudes, beliefs, and experiences learned through social interaction. Psychosexual adjustment emerges from this same organization, and in a general way mirrors one's level of satisfaction with self. The tasks are also largely the same, but are generally more complicated owing to the addition of the sexual component.

## PEER RELATIONSHIPS

The peer group provides the opportunity to learn how to interact with others. Successful interaction provides the broad range of positive experiences that build self-esteem. In the classroom or lecture hall, the learning is formal in the sense that it is directed; a fairly large percentage of formal learning is by rote. At home the learning is partly formal and partly informal; for the most part the learning that one receives at home is ideational, only very small amounts being learned by rote. There is an age hierarchy in both of these places of learning that ensures, for the most part, that progress is assessed by an "authority" figure employing for the most part a recognized and reputable system of grading. The learning that takes place in the peer group is not age related, nor is it formal. It is best described as relational in that it follows a pattern rather than specifics. When the "teaching" is done by peers, so also is the assessment. One significant aspect of peer assessment that makes it quite different from teacher or parental assessment is that it is frequently neither fair nor objective, that is, "how the boy rates with the group" is frequently nothing more than a judgment of how well he plays baseball or soccer. Often paradoxical, a boy's learning from his peers is probably best described as perceptual because it is inevitable that he will begin to make his judgments of people as well as events through the perceptions of others.

The influence of the peer group as a socializing agent cannot be equaled once the child's world has moved beyond his nuclear or extended family. The child who assimilates easily into the group experiences little of the rejection felt by the child who does not assimilate, or the one who does not easily assimilate. Each group has its cues and responses, behaviors and attitudes that are stressed and those that must be avoided. The newcomer must also be able to evaluate leadership within the group, and entry is generally marked by a willingness to follow the leader. For the most part, this means that anyone entering the group must imitate the verbal and nonverbal behavior of the dominant member or members. In this process, recognition is given to the dominant position and signals that the newcomer is ready and willing to obey the rules and procedures already set into place. The dominant member, in turn, signals approval by word or by deed, and the first stage of integration into the group is negotiated. Subsequent stages follow similar patterns.

In the event the newcomer does not earn the approval of the dominant member, approval will not be forthcoming and the group will close ranks behind the leader. Typically, the leader in either a small or large group remains as leader until and unless some dramatic event causes a shift. The dominant member, or leader, tends to exercise his dominance as long as the group stays together. While the dominant member in the larger group usually does remain as leader over a long period of time, shifts of allegiance among the members can bring about new leadership. Positions of leadership immediately below that of the dominant member are subject to change, and it is to this level of leadership that one can safely aspire.

Shifts in relationships can bring about changes in the power and structure of the group, and so it is in this social body that the child first experiences the reality of the "dominant leader" and the "submissive follower." His peer group can teach him to be independent, but it can also teach him to be dependent. Schoenberg and Preston (1983) noted that "dominance and submission are . . . concepts with characteristic indices moving across a continuum" (p. 76). And Luft (1970) stated that "the behavior is reciprocal, i.e., the one who communicates dominance tends to induce its complement, submission, in the other. Similarly, submissive behavior tends to induce dominant behavior in the other" (p. 52). The rules must be learned if membership is to be attained, but there is a risk that some of the lessons, such as submissive-dominant behavior, might be learned too well. That is, if submission to the leadership of the most active member is the ongoing price of membership, at what cost will the tactic be unlearned when it is no longer useful? Perhaps the better question might be, "Can it be unlearned?" And once an individual becomes comfortable in his dominance of his peer group, will it be a problem for him to accept a lesser role? The "natural leader" who no longer leads can be a pathetic figure. The influence of the peer group at times complements the moral and ethical training the boy has learned from his family, but it is far more likely that these new influences will directly or indirectly contradict the learnings of his rather brief lifetime. Conflict is the result, and how the lad handles it is closely related to age.

When the child is very young, the physical closeness he has with members of his family will work to ensure the preeminent influence of the family. Later, when he is old enough to move away from actual physical dependence on his family, it is almost inevitable that the influence of his group will equal or surpass the influence of his family. It is also likely that the age of the boy determines the long-term consequences of conflict. For example, the very young boy is likely to experiment with deception as a way of managing the ambivalences of his situation, telling untruths to his family on the one hand and to his friends on the other. He may not recognize the consequences of his actions: in a very real sense, he may not appreciate that either exaggeration or hiding behind an untruth is wrong. It is also likely that his coping behavior will be so transparent that his father or mother will be able to help him negotiate the ambivalent affect. If he isn't helped, the risk is that he will become masterful in the use of deception and possibly grow comfortable with its use. Becoming comfortable probably means that the youth will learn to mask the way he really feels, be able to disguise what he truly believes, and learn that he can be successful in manipulating the truth. In a very real sense, lying is a skill; and like other skills, it can be learned. Whether or not it is either good or appropriate to learn the skill is irrelevant.

The subculture of the peer group exacts conformity in matters of dress and behavior. Peers are called by different names at different developmental levels: friends, buddies, colleagues. The group is sometimes referred to as a gang; at other times it is termed a club or fraternity.

## SELF-PERCEPTION: THE EARNING
## OF RECOGNITION

Membership in a group is an important first step in belonging, but the manner or style in which one is accepted is more critical.

For the most part, the early stages of membership will be a time in which the new member will be assessed and evaluated. The status of membership, that is, his initial standing within the group, will be determined within a relatively short time. Subsequent events can raise or lower status, but change is the variation and not the rule. For most group members, their entry level will continue to delineate position and rank for as long as they stay with the group. It is within this context that external assessment and evaluation is termed recognition, and it is within this same context that the way one is recognized by peer associates is certain to determine the concept one forms of self.

Wideman and Clarke (1987) have written that a positive self-image (concept) "is fundamental to the well-being of the individual" (p. 24). They suggest the following as key principles: (1) the self-image is part of a larger personally held belief system; (2) the self-image shapes our experiences; (3) the self-image strives to maintain its self-consistency; (4) beliefs that are central to the self-image are harder to change; and (5) the self-image manifests itself in self-talk. Strang (1957) defined the basic self-concept "as the individual's perception of his abilities and his status and roles in the outer world," but argued that self-perception is a transitory construct referenced to the "immediate current situation" (p. 68). It is this transitory character of self-perception that enables the individual to continually modify his behaviors and attitudes so as to have them better conform to those that he believes others expect from him. This image of self, that is, the self-concept that emerges out of *perception* of recognition, will change throughout the several stages of development, primarily through variables such as the variety and intensity of personal interactions, the kinds and levels of anxieties with which he has to cope and the success he has in negotiating them, and his private assessment of personal worth.

Despite widespread denial, physical appearance continues to be one of the most heavily weighted considerations in the way people appraise one another. In recent years a number of concerned groups have expended a great amount of time and energy trying to educate people away from the notion that physical appearance is important. But reindoctrination efforts have met with selective successes at best: the severely handicapped individual is no longer singled out for close scrutiny, and is rarely asked questions that are blatantly insensitive. But for the most part, people continue "to judge a book by its cover"; and for the most part, the "cover" for a male is the way he looks. A strong and handsome male is scored higher than one who is neither strong nor handsome; coordination scores more points than awkwardness, the quick learner more than the slow. In addition, attractiveness earns the kind of positive recognition basic to the development of a healthy concept of self.

Demands of membership vary from group to group, which in theory makes it possible to change from one to the other. But not always. Gangs in particular require ongoing affiliation and inflict punishment on those who try to leave. Although gangs may be notorious in this regard, there is a price of one kind or another to be paid by any member who opts out of a group. Neighborhood groupings of small children are random by virtue of logistical proximity, becoming less so with the passing of time. In adolescence, increased mobility affords an opportunity for broader scope. With greater choice, the individual can elect to associate with those who can provide him the measure of personal recognition rewarding to his emotional well-being.

## INTEGRATION OF EXPERIENCE

According to English and English (1958), experience is best defined as "actual living through an event or events. . . . Experience is not static; it connotes activity, process, happening, doing" (pp. 194–95). It is an extremely broad concept, which can include formal/informal learning on the one hand and skills acquisition on the other. Experience is often reputed to be the best teacher; the reason this is so is somewhat obscured, but the words imply that one learns best those practical things to which one is exposed. Some experiences are good, others are bad; some teach what to do, others teach what not to do. Horrocks (1969) used the term "experience synthesis" to explain the principle of closure and stated that synthesis "involves both internal sensation and exterior experience and leads to the need to integrate this synthesis with the whole matrix of past experience. . . . Such integration . . . enables man to make sense of his past, his present, and his future" (p. 119). It is essential to remember that the individual has complete control of integration through a process of intrapsychic reaction management. In the first instance the person will determine whether the experience is valid and/or reasonable; in the second he will elect to interpret the meaning through his subjective filter; in the third he will determine to some extent how the experience can or should affect him; and in the fourth he will make a conscious decision whether to let significant others know the degree to which he has been affected. His attitudes and behaviors will be organized to the extent that he is successful in managing the experience effect.

Adolescent males in particular are under great pressure to conform to societal expectations of what a male should or should not be. The real problem is that adolescent males, no less than "society," have no real notion of what a male should or should not be, and as a result are forced into constructing their own notions. As might be expected, some become caricatures of masculinity, exaggerating those traits and characteristics they assume to be typical of male behavior. The way the individual understands the experiences of peer associates confirms his own perceptions; for example, overly aggressive behavior is internalized only if the group places a premium on it.

In general, integrating experience into one's personal frame of reference is a particularly critical developmental task for children and adolescents because it establishes the pattern that will carry into the adult years.

## MANAGEMENT OF PHYSICAL AND INTELLECTUAL GROWTH

In the larger sense, a person manages growth by coming to terms with it: accepting is one option, rejecting is another. Without due consideration, the thesis seems faulty. The question arises, in such a matter is it possible to either accept or reject? The answer: observe how people behave. Tall persons slouch, the short put on platform shoes. In a general sense, adolescent males are enthusiastic about physical growth because it is confirmation of approaching manhood. Still, and even with this as the given, physical growth exacts its pound of emotional flesh. A rapid spurt of growth might cause the adolescent boy to be clumsy or awkward, but in a general sense growth is a plus factor. The adolescent who doesn't grow has the problem. When physical growth is developmentally delayed, the adolescent boy tends to internalize feelings of negative self-worth. Blos (1941) wrote,

> The late developing boy or the boy showing inappropriate sex development is handicapped in his social development on account of group discrimination. It has been observed that changes in physical status are followed by a changed attitude of the group; thus, a boy with retarded maturation was long an outsider until a spurt of growth set in which subsequently led to his smooth absorption into the group. (p. 253)

Perhaps it all comes down to how the boy will suffer the torments and the teasing from his friends; the boy larger than his peers has the size-advantage that usually enables him to put an end to the teasing. The smaller lad will not have that physical option, so unless he finds some other way to fend off his badgerers he will continue to be tormented. At this stage of development, almost any deviation from the norm will cause concern, embarrassment, or shame. The physical aspects of sex assume a new level of importance; the adolescent is observing the physical presence of others, and in turn will likely become preoccupied with how others are perceiving him, his body, and his physical development. The adolescent boy will develop a different level of appreciation for females and will probably become very conscious of the way girls of his acquaintance are developing. He will also be intensely interested in the physical development of his male buddies and will begin to attach a special significance to penis size.

His newly discovered physical interest in girls is shared by his buddies, and the male peer group spends an inordinate amount of time talking about them. He is comfortable talking about his newly found interest in girls. He is not at all comfortable even thinking about his interest in males. He may be especially curious about how other males look when they're nude, and this bothers him. It does not occur to him that his male buddies are equally curious. He knows or thinks he knows that his buddies do not have this kind of interest, a level of thinking that might lead him to question the direction of his own sexuality. He may have absolutely no doubt that he's normal, but he fears being labeled deviant.

> Actually, a guy can wonder if he's homosexual simply because girls don't turn him on the way he *thinks* they should. It might even be the reverse side of the coin. He might not turn the girls on the way he *thinks* he should. A man can pick up homosexual patterns of behaviour in this manner purely by default. (Schoenberg, 1975, p. 251)

Sex may be the big worry, but there are other concerns as well. Appearance is important: facial features are especially important. Skin blemishes become a major concern, and the belief that they are brought on by masturbation brings on a higher level of anxiety. Height is a worry, and so is weight. He worries about his strength and the size of his chest. Shoulders are a problem: are they too narrow? The real bottom line is that there is no shortage of things for him to worry about.

Intellectual growth presents a completely different set of problems for him. Observation and experience provide support to the view that adolescent males generally do not like to be thought of as intellectually superior, and many work very hard to ensure they are not so labeled. However, and to a large extent, the area of expertise matters. Demonstrating knowledgeability in sports is the first among equals. It is okay to be good in math or chemistry or physics, but active participation in sports turns the okay into a plus. Demonstrating interest or ability in languages, especially English, risks the label of "brain." Interest in the social sciences is only marginally better.

The developmental task is that of building a system of concepts that will enable the adolescent to pattern the way he orders his view of the world. The sense grows that building a system of beliefs is an essential component of homeostasis. For those young men who have been given a strong foundation in behavioral and attitudinal ethics, the process is mostly agreeable in that it tends to reinforce an already well-developed ego structure. But those who for one reason or another did not internalize these codes of ethics, the process may prove to be arduous owing to an absence of guidelines on the one hand and a lack of confidence in self on the other.

## SOCIAL GROWTH AND
## PSYCHOSEXUAL INTEGRATION

Several decades before Tiger popularized the principle of bonding, Schoeppe, Haggard, and Havighurst (1953) wrote that boys were more likely than girls to achieve emotional independence and a mature sex role from interaction with their fathers. These same investigators stressed the importance the father plays in helping his son develop a strong moral code. Within a developmental sequence, the father's influence generally begins to wane as the boy becomes mobile and develops interactive relationships with his peers. Generally, if the father has forged a strong relationship with his son during the years of childhood, his teachings will have lasting effect. However, this does not mean that the lessons learned will not be bent or made subject to a differing interpretation in subsequent time frames.

Goldberg (1976) suggested four phases in the development of buddy-ship. They are: (1) the manipulative phase; (2) the companionship phase; (3) the friendship phase; and (4) the buddyship phase. In my view it would be useful to add two additional phases, that is, affiliation and exploration, both of which would precede the others.

Affiliation is the first phase, categorized by recognition of a mutual interest. As one example of affiliation, consider the strategies that travelers use to seek out others from their home state or town. They might have very little in common with each other, but the very fact that they share a bond in residence provides a measure of kinship when they find themselves in a distant locale. In this example, change in location provides the focus of interest. There is always a focus of interest, some form of common denominator, whenever people take up with each other. For adolescents, the focus or common denominator is shared interests, shared concerns. In broad context, this focus or common denominator provides the acceptable reason for a contact that otherwise simply might not happen; adolescent males in particular are made to feel keenly aware that social codes define the rules for encountering, especially the initial ones.

The exploration phase follows affiliation. Exploration provides the time as well as the opportunity for each to make a tentative assessment of the other. When these assessments are mutually positive, the friendship process gets under way.

The next phase is the manipulative, and it is here that the parameters of friendship begin to be negotiated. This can be a period of time when the newfound friends seem to be spending more time in arguing than actually getting along, but each has an agenda that delineates his position and serves to establish conditions for friendship. Each instinctively works to resolve the issue of dominance. Eventually, the parameters are set into place.

Testing the parameters, as well as broadening and expanding them, are the developmental tasks met with in the companionship phase. This phase marks the terminal point for those relationships that are not strong or enduring enough to last. However, those relationships that do survive and become comfortable are acknowledged as friendships, and the penultimate phase has been set in place. The final phase in the schema, buddyship, cements the male bond.

Buddyship goes beyond friendship and describes the kind of close personal interaction that comes but several times throughout a lifetime. The warmest of friendships tend to come and go, but buddyship is eternal and transcends time and distance. A man will have many friends through the years, but it is unlikely that he will ever have more than three or four guys he can think of as buddies.

## IN SEARCH OF AWARENESS

Good psychosexual adjustment means successful integration of the several dimensions of personality, that is, the emotional, the psychological, the social, the physical, the intellectual, and the sexual. Influences are reciprocal and carry the potential for support as well as for sabotage. Thomas Fuller's (1608–61) advice, "make not a bosom friend of a melancholy soul: he'll be sure to aggravate thy adversity, and lessen thy prosperity," emphasizes the reciprocity involved between emotionality and sociability; "a strong mind in a strong body" underscores the positive interaction between the physical and the intellectual. The influence that each dimension exerts on the individual likely parallels its relative strength within the personality configuration.

Schoenberg and Preston (1983) argued that "the way in which people develop their sexual self-concept is probably no different in substance from the manner in which the total self-concept is developed, but the subtleties of sex-role conditioning provide additional stumbling blocks" (p. 222). "Stumbling block" is generalized to refer to problems associated with sexual development, but the term could be used as well when referencing a specific, for instance, the youth who is immobilized around girls because he believes that girls find him unattractive.

Beauty (or handsomeness) influences one's sexual self-concept, but so does the size of the breast (or penis). Social skills are an assist in even the most casual of sexual encounters. The absence of social skills provides a fertile field for the growth of a belief in personal self-inadequacy on a sexual plane. Whether one participates in sports, dances well, or even dresses in accordance with the prevailing fashion for the respective age group are all important in one's identification of the sexual self, and the role that the sexual self can play. If one's perception of one's own sexual self is ambivalent, then the sexual self-concept will not be as sound as it should be. The number of factors, and variables, by which one person judges his/her sexuality relative to others is limitless . . . sexuality is the most unique of all personal identities, and thus no aspect of it can ever be compared in any kind of measurement, be it absolute or relative. (Schoenberg and Preston, 1983, p. 222)

Identification is likely the most important variable for strong psychosexual adjustment. Identification with gender is not innate; it is conditioned, and therefore must be learned. The adolescent male identifies with an older male and in such a way internalizes gender-appropriate behavior. As a concept, masculinity is passed on from one generation to the next: in a specific sense, from father to son; in a more general one, it is the heritage that men transmit to boys. In Western societies the rites of passage have never been as clearly demarcated as those of more primitive societies, but rites exist nevertheless. Stronger in the past, the remaining rites are in danger of being removed altogether owing primarily to issues arising from family disintegration. It is unlikely that civilized society can continue to be civilized if role models for males are absent or are in fact "demented anti-heroes" who can "get their act together" only when they're drunk or stoned.

Through competition the young male develops awareness of his physical power, of his strengths and of his weaknesses. He will learn to compete against himself in solo athletic activities and against others in team sports, and when the competition is healthy he will be helped to develop a real sense of his physical self. It is valuable for him to learn of his physical capabilities, but a more important undertaking may be to ensure that whatever physical strength he has becomes harnessed to an intellectual identity that stresses moral and ethical principles. Competition and other forms of assertive behavior are important to self-definition, and thus are essential for the youth striving to come to terms with himself. The individual who does not learn to channel or direct his behavior through healthy competition limits his behavioral repertoire and is unlikely to be effective in a really broad range of personal interactions. This will be so because his behavioral repertoire is apt to be limited to exaggerated masculinity on the one hand or wimpish indecisiveness on the other.

There is another, more expressive way to explain the correlation between (lack of) competition and (limited) behavioral repertoire. Farrell (1975) used the phrase "narcissism of the penis" to argue that man's sexuality is penis-centered. Because of this specific focus, the male adolescent who has not been taught to take pride in his masculinity, that is, his penis, neither learns nor becomes comfortable with physical competition. Sexton (1969) explains, "The active rebels, as well as the passive hippie protesters are often middle-class boys who have been feminized by schools, dominant mothers, and controls that keep them in swaddling clothes" (p. 4). It does seem reasonable to theorize that extreme positions on any continuum of masculinity grow out of incomplete understanding of one's sexual self. For example, the feminized male might be acting out because his situation provided little opportunity for gender identification. At the other end of the continuum, the overly aggressive male whose behavior is at best a caricature of masculinity is probably acting out his fantasy of how a man should behave. Extremes of behavior are characteristic of inadequate role identification.

Integration of the dimensions of personality is the first developmental objective and is essential to the building and maintenance of a healthy sex role identity. The male builds on his agenda, the female builds on hers. One gender has a penis, the other does not; a turn of the phrase might say that one gender has a vagina, and the other does not. If one is male, he has the option in a psychological or emotional sense to accept or reject his penis; most men accept. The female has the same option to accept or reject her vagina.

Freud wrote about penis envy to describe the young girl's reaction to a first awareness that she does not have this external appendage. Becoming aware that she does not have a penis should lead to a second level of awareness, that is, that her vagina was intended as a sheath for the penis, which in a sexual sense made her the equal partner of the male. Penis envy is a statement of fact, not necessarily a statement of a condition.

But the male does have a penis. The penis does represent male sexuality, so in that sense it is essential for a man to take inordinate pride in the sheer possession of it. Roszak and Roszak (1969) wrote that males want to assert the primacy of their aggressive organ, but it is difficult to understand what the authors mean by the observation. Having a penis guarantees nothing in the way of behavior. Still, throughout his life, the male who is well adjusted in the psychosexual sense is keenly aware of his masculinity, that is, the power of his penis. And perhaps this is what Roszak and Roszak meant to say. As the boy grows into young manhood, and subsequently to middle and old age, the meaning of the phrase undergoes a sometimes sharp redefinition.

It is unlikely that the adolescent in his early teen years invests his sexuality into actual physical strength. Although he recognizes a relationship of the one with the other, his notion is more likely to be that puberty and physical growth just happen to coincide. His developing body forces him to become aware of a sexual appetite; he develops a concern that his penis might be smaller than those of his friends, but for the most part sexual interest per se has no specific focus. The adolescent in his later teen years continues to be interested in the size of his muscles and the degree to which he is coordinated, but the most significant event in this period of growth is awareness that his sexuality, that is, the power of his penis, controls other facets of his being. Physical attractiveness, which may include physical strength, will likely become far more important. Although young adult males appear to measure penis power only in those areas most conspicuously associated with sexual energies and athletic ability, many begin to develop the sense that sexuality per se will be a major influence in vocational choice and avocational interest. For the most part, the pattern set will be the pattern followed; the male entering into his twenties must meet the developmental task of refining the experiences of his youth into the personal code that can give purpose and stability to his existence. His successes will be measured by the amount of purposeful direction that personal control allows him to sustain, and this will be quite literally the story of his life. Success in business or vocation may come to represent the musculature of his youth; if success does not happen, he may find an acceptable substitute.

Peer and associational relationships no less than those of marriage and family emerge out of acceptance of a psychosexuality whose beginnings emerged out of significant earlier relationships. Lidz (1968) wrote,

> since the general identity and its accompanying roles are so dependent upon the ways which parents relate to the child, interact with one another, and regard themselves, it becomes apparent that all sorts of variations in gender identity and in security and stability . . . can develop. Because the entire pattern of a person's relationships will

be carried out in accord with his sex, the gender identity will have far-reaching repercussions. (pp. 217–18)

It is not possible, neither would it be wise, for a man to view his life separate and apart from his gender, or the influence of that gender.

# 9

# Situational Ethics
# for Work and Play

A human being is not one thing among others; *things* determine each other, but *man* is ultimately self-determining. What he becomes—within the limits of endowment and environment—he has made out of himself. In the concentration camps, for example, in this living laboratory and on this testing ground, we watched and witnessed some of our comrades behave like swine while others behaved like saints. Man has both potentialities within himself; which one is actualized depends on decisions but not on conditions.

—Viktor Frankl,
*Man's Search for Meaning*

Theories of delinquent behavior generally focus on the person, the situation, or the person in the situation. Scientists and scientist-practitioners may subscribe to one theory or perhaps in some instances a mix of theories, and generally respect those who have arrived at theoretical positions differing from their own. In this one respect, theories of delinquent behavior do seem to stand alone: a few professionals pontificate as if they had cornered the market on revealed truth.

## THE ROLE OF LINGUISTICS IN
## THE FORMATION OF ETHICS

As with other basic issues, situational ethics are learned by teachings both direct and indirect. Ethics are internalized when the individual believes them to be consonant with his situation and value system, and become integrated only after a period of trial-and-error experimentation. In common with other basic issues, the process by which one learns right from wrong is extraordinarily complex. The parent rearing a child looks for straightforward answers to puzzling questions and becomes impatient when he learns that answers are usually no less puzzling than the questions. Perhaps "impatient" is not the best word. In a real sense people are frustrated to learn that instead of one answer there may be many; or worse, none at all.

It is not difficult to understand pressure for the simple answer, but there are problems. The most obvious one is that the simple answer tends to circumvent the issue rather than resolve it. Another problem is that the gestalt is more than an aggregate of easily understood parts—that is, a man is the *sum* of his parts. Moreover, demystification labels but it does not explain. It might, for example, seem to remove a bit of the mystery and help to explain psychopathic rage by referring it to the general group of behaviors that bear the label of temporary insanity. This is somewhat illusory however because temporary insanity is more a legal artifact than a psychological reality. Schoenberg and Preston (1983) explain more fully that such a classification does not illuminate the underlying psycho-pathology. They refer to the issue of specifically certifying someone as temporarily insane as follows:

> Usually this kind of plea is used in a courtroom as a rationale to explain an outburst of violent behavior. The plea arises as a result of an attorney's willingness to use any kind of ploy to win release for his/her client, but professional workers have not been seen to resist too strenuously being used to achieve dubious ends. This is not to say that "temporary insanity" does not exist, not by that term, of course. Rage, ingestion of alcohol or drugs, etc., do bring about reduction of the control of internal censoring mechanisms, but the inability to control one's actions, whatever the reason, is no justification for asocial, antisocial, or violent behavior. For that matter, this type of reasoning can be extended to include any kind of behavior. For example, driving one's car through an intersection in violation of a red traffic light can be said to be a result of temporary insanity. Insanity, as a word, has never had any meaning in the psychological sense; every time the plea is used, public credulity is stretched nearer to the inevitable breaking point. (Schoenberg and Preston, 1983, p. 125)

Some people will argue, albeit foolishly, that the use of imprecise language presents no real problem for the average man because his work does not require him to be a skilled linguist. These same people, I believe, would argue that life is too short for the average man to try to be everything that he can possibly be.

Some linguists argue that imprecision in language can be justified because language itself is live and growing. The argument is compelling to a point, but it can become disingenuous. A new, possibly radically different meaning for a particular word is acceptable, for instance "gay." Sometimes the meaning of a word is expanded, as in "blitzkrieg." Word changes such as these are indeed proof that the language is alive, and that it is growing to meet the challenge of a different age. But change in meaning for a word is not the same as linguistic imprecision. The following paragraph demonstrates how one particular term has been rendered almost meaningless.

> Since no one can define mental health, or its scope, all kinds of irrelevancies are brought in under the umbrella. Consider the following: The child is not to be disciplined because of unknown (probably) deleterious emotional effects; abortion on demand must be made available because people (men and women alike!) are too short-sighted to use birth control methods; welfare types must be supported because to insist that they work at a job could be emotionally injurious. And so on. (Schoenberg and Preston, 1983, p. 125)

It is not a matter of the one being a word and the other a concept; and in the case of a concept, it is not always a matter of honest difference in either opinion or interpretation. In point of fact, opinion-giving is subjective interpretation.

Some level of conceptual organization is required to understand what is mean by the term "sexual harassment." In general, the term means that someone, usually a woman, is the unwilling recipient of unwanted sexual attention. Can it mean more? Amiel (1984) reports on the deliberations of a tribunal set in place by the Canadian Human Rights Commission:

> According to the tribunal's written judgment, MacBain was guilty of creating a "poisoned atmosphere." The tribunal wrote that "sexual harassment that does not otherwise adversely affect the woman's employment may nonetheless be discrimination on the basis of sex if it simply makes the work environment unpleasant." The tribunal

tried to define what that meant. Its members suggested that sexual harassment occurs if "a reasonable person ought to have known that such behavior was unwelcome." Alas, in its honesty the tribunal detonated the argument when it went on to state that what a reasonable woman might see as sexual harassment may not be seen as harassment by a reasonable man. (p. 9)

Subjective interpretation is remarkably easy. It becomes insidious if left unchallenged by the apathetic or the indifferent. The redefining process occurs over an extended period of time. The process can be deliberate, and it can be orchestrated. Amiel (1984) asks, "Surely it is not an offence if an employer acknowledges the gender of an employee with a remark," and the obvious answer is that it should not be. The obvious conclusion to be drawn from this observation is incredulity that this kind and level of fuzzy thinking is even said aloud.

Why all this discussion about linguistic imprecision, evasion, and the like in a book dealing with masculinity? Part of the answer is furnished by Toffler (1971),

We are simultaneously experiencing a youth revolution, a sexual revolution, a racial revolution, a colonial revolution, an economic revolution, and the most rapid and deep-going technological revolution in history. We are living through the general crisis of industrialism. (p. 186)

We are living in difficult times and seem to lurch from one crisis to another. The rhetoric that resounds from each of the interest groups can sometimes be fairly heady stuff, meant more to proselytize than educate. American political theater hangs on the overkill; it may fascinate the world, but the by-product is worldwide loss of respect for American political institutions. In this context, one has to wonder if radical feminists are ever as militant as their stridency suggests. To be sure, it does not appear their message has appeal beyond a very narrow constituency.

The typical male response has been to ignore the critic and dismiss the criticism. Because men for the most part have not responded, male issues in general and masculinity in particular have received a less than favorable press. Complacency must end. In order for this to happen, there has to be a large increase in the number of male activists and a greater awareness of the issues. In other words, the first line of defense is to pay attention.

The times are changing, and men must change with them.

## DEFINING SELF: THE RULES AND THE TOOLS

In one important sense, *we are who we think we are*; in another, *we are what others think we are*. The typical man is neither the one nor the other, but rather an agreeable synthesis of the two. These standards guide the formation of self. The one is called assessment, the other perception.

It is likely that the individual forms assessment antecedent to perception, but the point is arguable. It does seem clear that since assessment most certainly influences all elements within the perceptual field, trying to form judgments of the opinion of others would be of highest priority. They are reciprocal, possibly cyclical in the sense that one is dependent on the other. In a theoretical sense, objective assessment requires accurate perception in the very same way that objective perception requires correct assessment. The importance of perception in self-assessment is abundantly clear. In a relative sense, a man will be unable to capitalize on a particular strength until and unless he perceives, recognizes, or otherwise becomes aware of his capability. The opposite condition is also true. When a man does not recognize or perceive a specific weakness, it is likely he will have to pay some price before he does come to recognize it. In this sense perception is a personalized phenomenon that may or may not reflect the extent to which the individual is in touch with himself and his surroundings: a surprising number of people seem to be afflicted with perceptual illusions. The individual may also realize he is deluding himself to some extent or another, but may believe he has very good reasons for the charade.

The quality of one's perception becomes a critical factor in determining the value that others assign to us. The notion that the introvert devalues and the extravert overvalues is simplistic; still the introvert must have grown inward for a reason. Belief that he does not rate well with significant others could be a factor. The spoken or written word forms the base for one level of perceptual awareness; body language or nonverbal communication forms the base for the second level. Nonverbal cues are often the more instructive for the not so obvious reason that people are not always altogether honest or frank. The man who believes himself to be deficient in picking up on the unspoken word would be well advised to enroll in a group specializing in sensitivity training.

The additional complication is that some people never get a really good handle on who they are, in the process sending out conflicted messages to others who may be trying to read them. Not knowing oneself in full measure is natural enough, but a man should study himself and learn everything that he possibly can. As well, it would seem that everyone wants to keep certain things away from common knowledge.

A parenthetical note must be added. The cause-and-effect relationship between lack of exercise and a flabby body is easier to grasp than the one between disciplined intellect and imprecise language; yet the principle is the same. A disciplined intellect enables a man to decide not only what he will integrate but also the extent to which he will or will not integrate, thereby allowing him to fashion and control his personal code of behavioral ethics.

## ETHICS: THE THIRD PARENT

If the first parent bonds the man and the second nurtures him, the third will most certainly determine his behavioral code, that is, his personal code of ethical conduct. The influence of the father and the mother may wane as the man grows older, but all things being equal, his personal code of ethics will be with him always.

Developmental stages are marked in large measure by the person or persons who either were the most significant or came to exercise the most influence. Initially it was the mother, then the mother and father, then the father, and lastly his peer group both in and out of school. The other individuals who exerted influence, such as teachers and coaches, were mostly incidental, and grew or waned in significance as a consequence of the youth's interests and abilities.

Behavioral scientists sometimes refer to societal influence as an entity separate and apart from family and peer associates. Every society has a culture to which its members are indoctrinated, in one way or another, by means both subtle and obvious. The imprint, that is, the impact of indoctrination efforts, does not always "take" in a positive sense; in other words, the man has the option of resisting as well as accepting. The extent to which an individual interacts with others in his environment is likely to be the most accurate measurement of societal influence, and it is also likely that the man whose interactions tend to be upbeat and positive will be influenced in a more constructive way than the one whose interactions are generally marked by hostility or conflict. In much the same way that each individual is distinctive because of the unique way his ego resolves conflict between the id and the superego, each of us has arrived at our distinct personality base because of the impact of those who influenced us in successive developmental stages. In successive stages, significant others have contributed to the repertoire of interactive skills.

But in this context it must be remembered that a human being is not a sponge. No man has to be influenced against his will. There is an element of reciprocity between influence per se and receptivity to influence per se that enables the individual to maintain control over the process. The choice must be conscious, based on the certain knowledge that one is able to accept or reject. Even when the choice is extremely difficult, it is still his to make. Some social theorists will take issue, arguing that environmental influences can impact to such a degree that the individual is effectively robbed of choice. The point has some validity, but to put decision-making in its proper perspective the individual should be able to fully appreciate the impact of intrapersonal conflict. It could very well be a matter of holding out for the light at the end of the tunnel.

## TESTING REALITY I:
## WE ARE WHO WE THINK WE ARE

It is true that a man is the sum total of *all* his experiences, but that is only part of his story. The other part, equally important, is the success he has had in integrating *all* of these experiences into an emotional and behavioral repertoire selectively geared to his interactive needs. In whatever measure, success is translated into an operational vision of self that serves to promote whatever he perceives as his best interests. This operational vision of self is sometimes termed self-image or self-esteem, perhaps self-worth or self-regard. Regardless of the name it is given, it is important to know that it frequently operates on the principle of the self-fulfilling prophecy.

On a slightly different level, a man's vision of self emerges from the way he was taught to think in an egoistic or self-centered manner. The specific process begins with the child's parents. They soothed and played with him, and through a process of trial and error he stumbled on ways to demonstrate behaviors that elicited additional pleasure. As the elicited behavior in its turn becomes reinforced, it is integrated as part of the child's behavioral repertoire. The primary bond with the father is probably the base on which the boy's ego begins to build his own concept of gender identity, which in the course of time becomes fused with an ever-expanding sense of personal awareness. Consciously, but also unconsciously, the child begins to play roles. He is able to identify these roles as son, brother, nephew, or playmate, and develops an awareness that each role may require from him a marginally different kind of performance. In addition, he begins to form critical self-appraisal of each role-playing performance and will come to realize that he is able to perform well in some areas but not so well in others. In the end, and as a result of this critical self-appraisal,

the boy will begin to ascribe position for each role-play along a scale
ranging from good to bad, satisfactory to unsatisfactory. Practice as well
as refinement brings about change in positioning, but what is important
about the labeling is that it does tend to shape beliefs about himself that
become central to his personally held belief system. Cochran (1985) wrote,

> A role as a situation, as part of external reality, offers a viewpoint for
> construing the world. The role exists in relation to other roles, and so
> forms a role map. One can identify one's position, as if on a map of
> a territory, and see what might constitute an improvement of position.
> Or, like a chess position, one might note strengths and weaknesses,
> devising strategies and tactics for improving position or defending
> against vulnerability. But as soon as we speak of improvements,
> strategy, strengths, and weaknesses, we are presuming a stance one
> has taken. The role situation as mapped is the reality on which and
> within which one takes a position. (p. 33)

Role describes attitude and/or behavior, but its more important consequence may be that of predictor. Experience provides a level or awareness
of success, or possible failure, and it is this awareness or stance that risks
being translated into self-fulfilling prophecy. One's system of personally
held beliefs can influence behavior to a remarkable extent. Imagination
creates a visualized goal of what is possible and/or what is not possible.
Because feelings and emotions are the affective aspects of behavior, it is
not difficult to demonstrate the relationship between positive attitude and
successful performance. Thus the individual who adopts a stance of *not
being good at something* courts failure in the same way that the individual
who adopts a stance of *being good at something* courts success. Plato
regarded thinking as the soul in dialogue with itself: we might wish to
paraphrase it as the mind in dialogue with itself, but in either sense the
message is clear. The person who we think we are controls a large part of
our destiny.

## TESTING REALITY II:
## WE ARE WHAT OTHERS THINK WE ARE

The importance of thinking in a positive way about oneself was the
subject of the previous section. But man does not live in a vacuum; from
childhood on he is accustomed to interact regularly with all kinds of
people, in all kinds of relationships. Man is a social organism, and social
forces exert powerful influence on his behavior. It is likely that the most

powerful social force of all is the reaction to what we perceive as judgments from family, peers, and associates. We are, to a very large degree, what others think we are. Every individual has control to some extent of the way he presents himself to significant others. It is well to keep this in mind, because no man should be a reed bending at the mercy of the wind.

The ability to fathom what others are thinking or feeling is a skill that some seem to learn better than others. Perception is a two-way process in that the individual not only acts, but also reacts. A learned insensitivity may be part of the problem; men are not genetically programmed to be less sensitive than women, but the truth of the matter is that some of their social programming can get in the way of perceptual awareness. Fasteau (1974) described the problem as follows:

> In a world which tells men they have to choose between expressiveness and manly strength, this characterization may be accurate. Most of the men who talk personally to other men *are* those whose problems have gotten the best of them, who simply can't help it. Men not driven to despair don't talk about themselves, so the idea that self-disclosure and expressiveness are associated with problems and weakness becomes a self-fulfilling prophecy. (p. 11)

Goldberg (1976) is more explicit.

> The male has become anaesthetized and robotized because he has been heavily socialized to repress and deny almost the total range of his emotions and human needs in order that he can perform in the acceptable "masculine" way. Feelings become unknown, unpredictable quantities, expressions of which threaten him and make him feel vulnerable. By the time he is a mature adult he also has undoubtedly surrounded himself with a family environment that has a heavy stake in his continuing non-feeling and in subtle ways reinforces his functioning as a well-oiled machine. Should inner feelings come pouring through, particularly on a continuing basis, in the form of powerful emotional needs, fears, and conflicts, he would be encouraged to get professional help to patch up and help him regain emotional control. (p. 55)

Perception and expressiveness are not unrelated, because it is abundantly clear that the nature and quality of individual expression can and does affect the nature and quality of perception. In this context, it is useful for a man to understand that for an effect there has to be a cause. It logically follows that when the cause is identified, it is open to remedy. Understanding this simple connection will be of critical import to the male who has difficulty expressing himself. Learning to express oneself involves an element of risk-taking for sure, but for the typical male the risks become manageable when they are considered separate and apart from the complexity of the masculine value system. In general, perception and expression are skills that first may have to be learned and subsequently refined.

The notion of the self-fulfilling prophecy, so important a consideration in internal deliberations related to *who we think we are*, is no less important in determining the person *who others think we are*. The notion may be more complicated owing to the volley effect, that is, reciprocity between two levels of perception, and as a result may be more difficult to manage. For example, few would argue the point that the attitudes and expectations of significant others can influence one's level of performance; it is equally the case that few would argue that one's own attitude and/or expectation can influence one's level of performance. However, the problem goes beyond the usual suggestions of expectation and perception.

There is no clear distinction between the short term and the long term in either expectation or perception. The question might be phrased thus: When does the occasional expectation of success or failure become generalized into the routine expectation? The answer might be, when the pattern has been set. That is a reasonable response, except the additional question might be: How long does it take to set the pattern? And on to infinity. The fact is that sooner or later an attitude will take over, and this attitude will affect the performance of the individual. The thoughtful individual will not allow others to impose their attitudes on him. It's a matter of keeping oneself in the driver's seat.

In order to defend oneself, it becomes useful to understand how easy it is to adopt an attitude of compliance. Winokur (1973) wrote,

> The final disadvantage is that the illness model reinforces the notion that . . . patients are sick, cannot really take care of themselves, and cannot take responsibility for their own behavior. If we convey the idea to a patient that he is sick, too disturbed to make decent decisions about himself, then we stand the risk of perpetuating his dependency and inadvertently encouraging him to manipulate his healthy therapist to take over his life. (p. 42)

The adolescent who is invariably the last player chosen for the team internalizes another's judgment that he cannot play the game very well. Using Winokur's sickness model, it is probable that this adolescent will begin to see himself as someone who cannot play the game very well and will act accordingly. There is no hidden agenda for player selection; the team wants to win the ballgame, so players are selected with that objective in mind. However, the cause is one thing; the effect, another. It is a difficult situation, but there are ways to handle it. It is not only a matter of playground supervisors emphasizing the importance of playing the game as opposed to the importance of winning. The rejected player should have it spelled out that being weak in athletics does not mean he will be weak in life.

## TESTING REALITY III: THE UNKNOWNS

Defending and preserving the integrity of the self-concept is the raison d'être for all behaviors and all attitudes, including those that are unknown or kept hidden.

It is unlikely that anyone would truly want his life to be an open book. Behaviors are not always commendable, attitudes not always praise-worthy. The bigot hides his bigotry, the weakling hides his weakness. Hidden behaviors and concealed attitudes are the psychic infrastructure for the unknowns.

Unknown behavior contains those behaviors and attitudes that the individual has made a conscious decision to conceal. Education as well as experience works to change attitudes, providing opportunity for the individual to move items out into the open if and when he elects to do so.

## SOME CONCLUSIONS ABOUT
## THE INFLUENCE OF ETHICS

A discriminating grasp of the bridge relationship between attitudes and behavior on the one hand and the building blocks of personal control and self-discipline on the other is essential to understanding the nature of a man's code of conduct. The average person introduces changes into his life on the basis of need, want, or interest. It is a fact of life that no one has complete control of his situation, that there are instances when learning to cope with a problem is the only available option. As well, codes of behavioral ethics set limits on what the person can do.

The desire to receive everything one wants to obtain—love, protec-tion, knowledge, material things—in a passive way from a source outside of oneself, develops in a child's character as a reaction to his experiences with others. If through these experiences the feeling of his own strength is weakened by fear, if his initiative and self-confidence are paralyzed, if hostility develops and is repressed, and if at the same time his father or mother offers affection or care under the condition of surrender, such a constellation leads to an attitude in which active mastery is given up and all his energies are turned in the direction of an outside source, from which the fulfillment of all wishes will eventually come. This attitude assumes such a passionate character because it is the only way in which such a person can attempt to realize his wishes. (Fromm, 1972, p. 319)

In addition, behavioral codes develop from interactive experiences with significant others. It is the exception for parents or significant others to have codes of ethics per se in mind when they begin to teach the child right from wrong, but of course this is the way the child acquires the learning. Parameters of the code will expand and become discriminative as the child matures. The process of acculturation continues through adolescence and into adulthood, becoming more or less fixed during this latter stage of emotional and physical development. When the horizons are narrow, the code will be narrow.

It is a mistake to conceptualize ethics in any kind of restrictive sense. Their effectiveness as behavioral guidelines is measured in terms of the degree to which they are useful in controlling maladaptive or counter-productive behaviors.

# 10

# Sexuality and Relationships

Only so far as a man is happily married to himself, is he fit for married life to another, and for family life generally.

—Novalis,
*Pseudonym of Friedrich von Hardenberg*

The state of wedlock produces a kind of lockjaw which prevents the victim from talking about his plight.

Kathryn Perutz,
*Marriage is Hell*

There are a number of ways for man to express his sexual nature.

The overwhelming majority of men marry, so for this overwhelming majority heterosexuality within the traditional monogamous marriage appears to be the norm. But evidence supports a belief that large numbers of married men are expressing their sexual nature outside the husband–wife relationship. It is not at all certain that men who report themselves as homosexual marry or remain married for any period of time, but bisexuality is a completely different matter. Moreover, it is a clinically accepted belief that most men masturbate without regard to marital status.

The traditional marriage remains the option of choice for most men. However, as Silverman (1981) notes, "the practice of cohabitation without the benefit or curse of civil and religious matrimonial sanction is statistically on the increase as an alternative life style. . . . Some couples consider themselves morally married, but for a variety of reasons defer the arrangement of legal marriage" (p. 55). Even so, and discounting those in the entertainment industry who adopt whichever life style is capable of generating the most publicity, the fact is that an increasing number of men and women are opting out of marriage. Now that the courts are making live-in partners legally responsible within the arrangement, it will be interesting to see if the number of people living common-law continues at its present rate.

## HOMOSEXUALITY

Homosexual relationships may not be typical, but neither are they terribly uncommon. Sexual encounters between males are often casual, one-occasion events. Gay males meet, engage in sexual activity, and part company. This is the kind of encounter described as casual sex, and it is arguably the most frequent expression in male homosexuality. In a historical sense, long-term relationships have not been the standard for gay male couples, but it is likely that the impermanence was the result of strong social disapproval. But as Guze (1992) points out, "over a short period of time, homosexuality was regarded by physicians primarily as a moral problem (a sin), then primarily a medical problem (a psychiatric disorder) and 'finally' as simply an alternate form of sexual orientation, requiring no intervention" (p. 7). As societal attitudes toward homosexuality have changed, the pattern for gay relationships has also changed. In sum, we may see long-term (or at least *short* long-term) relationships on the rise. Blair (1981) wrote,

> We know now, better than we ever have, that homosexuality is simply the *direction* of the sexual drive. As such, it should not be condemned or especially celebrated. It does need to be accepted as only a part, though a very important part, of an individual's life. It must be recognized that there are very destructive and undesirable effects when either homosexuals or others fail to accept the natural homosexuality which develops in many people. Likewise, it must be appreciated that there are positive results when both homosexuals and others learn to accept this natural homosexuality and get on with the living of the rest of their lives. (p. 140)

Earlier, Clark (1974) noted that the specter of homosexuality serves to complicate adult male interactions. In *A Strange Breed of Cat*, Jim described how it worked by saying that "I've been crapped on by so many straights and so many jerks who are trying to prove to themselves that they're straight" (Schoenberg, 1975, p. 127). An adolescent male is particularly vulnerable, and as a result will work to ensure that physical as well as emotional distance is maintained with male friends. Maintaining this distance sets up barriers in the way that men communicate and interact with each other. It is this specter, according to Clark (1974), that seems to be the dragon at the gateway of self-awareness, understanding, and acceptance of male–male needs.

> The dragon need not be at the gate. It is a monster that has been created by our society. Homosexuality is a reality but it need not be a monster. Since it is firmly chained to the gate at this point in the evolution of our culture, however, a man has few choices. He can blind himself to the dragon and be blind to what lies beyond the gate. He can stand far back from the dragon and settle for awareness that there is a barrier between himself and the gate that he is unwilling to confront. He can compulsively interact with the dragon. Or he can confront the dragon—find strength to admit homoerotic impulses, admit that he is a beautiful and impressive dragon (valued along with other things life has to offer, in addition) and pass through the gateway to self-awareness, understanding, and acceptance. (p. 100)

## BISEXUALITY

It is probably not accurate to categorize bisexuality as an option per se. One gets the sense that bisexuals do not generally communicate too much about themselves to others, and especially to their sexual partners. The direction of their sexual energies is toward males as well as females: bisexuals are rated midway, 3, on the Kinsey Heterosexual–Homosexual Rating Scale. In noting that the term is often mistakenly applied to homosexuals, Tollison and Adams (1979) defined bisexuality as "describing individuals who engage in both homosexual and heterosexual behavior, and who claim a permanent need and desire for relation with both sexes" (p. 202).

The argument that bisexuality is a cover for homosexuals is made by Festinger (1957), and others, who categorize the bisexual as "proving he is not homosexual" by involving himself in heterosexual encounters. Festinger suggested that bisexuals are able to achieve penile erections in heterosexual encounters through discrete use of homosexual fantasy. But some bisexuals argue that they do not make use of fantasy, homo- or hetero-; one does get the sense that bisexuals believe that their dual orientation serves their interests better than if they were single-sex directed.

The following bit of dialogue from *A Strange Breed of Cat* (Schoenberg,

1975, pp. 194–95) underscores this feeling. Mike, the bisexual in this all-male encounter group, is defending himself against Jim, a young homosexual, and Frank, who happens to have a heterosexual orientation but whose main thrust in the group emerges from the fact that he is a graduate student in psychology. The character Joe is probably the most typical male in the group. Joe is athletic, likable, attracted to girls and finds that they are attracted to him. Frank, who generally is either "lecturing" or "explaining," is doing a bit of both at the moment.

**Frank:** Let me explain, Rick. Mike's been playing a role all this goddamned time. You see, he's the happy bisexual of the group. Militant perhaps, but happy. Mike feels he has the best of two worlds going for him.

**Mike:** Right. I'm no narrow-minded bastard like you!

**Jim:** (*mimics*) Mike swings AC-DC.

**Joe:** Right. He talks about the rest of us feeling so goddamn superior. But all the time he's been coming on like I'm some kind of narrow-minded freak.

**Frank:** Not only you, Joe. He has the same contempt for Jim and Carlos that he has for you and me. That part of it hasn't shown through yet, and that's the part that Carlos is going to show us about him.

**Mike:** Oh, shit! You and your goddamned analysis. I don't feel like I'm superior to anybody in this room. Okay. I take girls to bed; I take boys to bed. I like them both in different ways. Does this make me superior to you?

**Frank:** Only because you think it does. You think that because the rest of us don't think your way that we are all narrow-minded as hell.

**Mike:** The only thing I say about all this, Mr. Analyst, is that I'm a hell of a lot more honest with my emotions than the rest of you. You shit all over yourself if you think about a man. It might work the reverse for Jim. I don't know. I think all of you have a lot to learn about yourselves.

In another place, and directly addressing this issue of superiority, Mike speaks out.

I know I've been accused by this group of feeling superior to everybody else. I reject that as a statement of fact, and I will continue to reject it. But what I will say about me is that I know myself quite well, and that usually I'm in fairly good control of my emotions. I think I learned long ago that when I was having a hassle with somebody or when I didn't understand somebody else's attitude towards me that if I really cared about what was going on, I'll examine me instead of trying to speculate about what was wrong with the other guy. And you know it works almost 100 percent of the time? (*Laughs loudly*) Of course there's always the exception like Todd was talking about. There was no way I could have taken the time to have figured that hassle out. But seriously, what you've got to do is figure out how much the person means to you. If he or she means something and it's worth your time, you start examining how you may be coming across and what you can do to improve the situation. If you decide the person means nothing to you, the answer is obvious. You just back away and write it off. There's no point in hassling unless a very solid principle is involved. If you go around uptight, it's your own bloody fault ninety percent of the time. And so that's what I'm saying about Frank. He obviously has felt beholden to authority all his life, and this is the first opportunity the poor bastard has had to challenge it. (*A Strange Breed of Cat*, pp. 216–17)

## MASTURBATION

Masturbation is a widespread practice. Schiller (1981) notes that 95 percent of all men report that self-stimulation is part of their sexual experience, that masturbation is commonly practiced in and out of marriage, and that people who are "better educated" are "more likely to masturbate than are less-educated persons perhaps because of the fact that better educated people are better informed and do not view it as a health hazard" (p. 68). In Western societies, some measure of guilt is typically experienced by the man who masturbates to orgasm, primarily because of the religious proscription against the practice. McCary (1973) wrote of the taboo,

> Much has been said about Onan's "spilling his seed on the ground" as recorded in Genesis. This story involved Onan's being ordered by God to marry his deceased brother's wife, as was the custom, and to have children by her. Onan refused to do so, apparently employing *coitus interruptus* as a birth control method, because any children born of the union would have borne his brother's name and not his own. God was angered by Onan's defiance of His orders and struck him dead. The misinterpretations of this story have had severe repercussions on Western sexual stability over the centuries. Onanism somehow became enlarged to imply a method of birth control. Furthermore, some time during the seventeenth century the "spilling of seed" and masturbation became equated, masturbation thenceforth being condemned as gravely sinful. (p. 10)

Nonetheless, and despite feelings of guilt, there is strong reason to believe that most men regularly masturbate to orgasm. A fairly regular regimen of masturbation by the single male can be accurately described as one of his options. For one reason or another, a man might not want to enter into a sexual relationship with some other person.

## CELIBACY

It is likely that the larger number of celibate males by far are to be found in the religious orders, but therapists acknowledge that the celibate life style is not as uncommon as one might suspect. It is as yet unclear whether the specter of Acquired Immune-Deficiency Syndrome (AIDS) will bring about an increase in the number of celibates. A highly disciplined man might persuade himself that remaining celibate affirms the measure of personal control he is able to exert upon himself; an extremely devout man might view it as a sign of spiritual fervor. McCary (1973) notes,

The writings of St. Augustine during the fourth century A.D. have probably had as much impact upon prevailing twentieth-century sexual attitudes as any other single force. In them he severely condemned premarital and extramarital sexual outlets, including bestiality, homosexuality, and, especially, masturbation. *In time the Roman Catholic Church came to idealize celibacy* [emphasis added] with the highest level of male achievement being total rejection of all life's pleasures, while women would expect to reach their greatest glory only through permanent virginity. (p. 11)

## MARRIAGE: THE OTHER SIDE
## TO THE BED OF ROSES

To introduce this discussion of marriage, it might be useful to again observe that "this is not meant to be a cynical chapter on marriage, but a realistic appraisal of the what and the why of contemporary marriages" (Schoenberg, 1981, p. 69). Two central questions are of particular interest: (1) what do people expect in marriage? and (2) why is there so much disappointment and failure?

In 1936, Westermarck wrote,

Marriage is not made for everybody, not attractive to everybody, nor good for everybody who embarks in it. It is the cause of much suffering; it is bleeding from a thousand wounds. As Stevenson said, "marriage is life in this—that it is a field of battle, and not a bed of roses." (p. 39)

A man entering into marriage does not expect marriage to be a cause for suffering, and most certainly not a field of battle. Men as well as women enter into marriage convinced that courtship will endure and that bliss will go on forever. Even those individuals who knew of problems in the relationship prior to marriage had abiding faith that they would disappear once the vows were said. The disappointment and failure emerge when either or both of the partners begin to realize that love, marriage, and happiness are not necessarily coexisting variables. Gordon and Meth (1990) write,

> When a man loves and commits to a woman, he finds ways to get closer that are comfortable and familiar to him, usually through the physical aspects of a relationship. Sexual intimacy is sometimes the sole means of how males express their affection for their partner, providing an acceptable means of emotional bonding. According to existing models of masculinity, a husband is allowed to depend on his wife for this. But for couples, sexuality can be the source of many marital battles. In our clinical practice we hear women express frustration over what they consider their husband's preoccupation with sex. Sexual intimacy may meet a man's needs but can simultaneously negate the woman's needs, who has other ways of expressing and giving love. This is one of the more common problems marital therapists face. Irreconcilable difference and marital dissolution are not unusual outcomes. (p. 74)

Schoenberg (1981) cautioned, "No contract should ever be entered into without clear-eyed, reasonable understanding and some foresight about the possible consequences. But that is not, alas, how literature, history, art and man have portrayed 'true love' and marriage—as though one necessitated the other" (p. 69). Part of the folklore of marriage is that the man and the woman will inevitably grow closer as a result of the union: if the woman is a nag, marriage will cure her; if the man is a drunk, he'll stop drinking in the face of his new responsibility. This is the theory, but the reality is generally quite different.

Silverman (1981) has written that "the psychological problems central for all of us regardless of sexual identity are the establishment and maintenance of self-esteem, the development of competence, the pursuit and development of intimacy with others, and the generation of a meaning for existence" (p. 44). It is while in pursuit of intimacy with others that men and women get caught up in the notion of romantic love; the problem is not with the notion of romance, but rather with the false assumptions that have grown up around the notion. Lederer and Jackson (1968) have listed the following as false assumptions:

1. That people marry because they love each other,
2. That most married people love each other,
3. That love is necessary for a satisfactory marriage (p. 7).

Romanticists, on the other hand, remain convinced that people fall in love "when the time is ripe," that they marry "for better or for worse," embark on a journey "to raise their family" in "a vine-covered cottage," and that "all live happily ever after." Realists regard this view of marriage as "pie in the sky" and would argue that there has to be more substance to the relationship than hopes and dreams. Arranged marriages operate on the premise that the man and woman fall in love as they get used to living with each other; that is, deep affection may be lacking at the outset, but the couple has the time, the opportunity, and are keenly aware of the commitment they owe the family in order to make the marriage work. Arranged marriages do not always result in happy and enduring relationships, but there is little evidence to suggest that the track record is any worse than those that have not been brokered. The notion of romantic love is that the couple falls in love and then gets to know each other. Church as well as civil ceremonies worked to cement the relationship, in effect ensuring that the couple tried to make a go of their marriage. However, the past several decades have brought about significant change in the view people have of marriage and most importantly divorce. The results of this more liberal attitude have been good for some in that there is less pressure to continue within an ailing relationship, but bad for others because they believe they have license to move in and out of marriage, with little or no thought given to consequence.

Feminists have argued for substantial role change within marriage. Komarovsky (1976) suggests the need for "more vivid models of egalitarian relationships" (p. 149), whatever this might mean. Others are more combative. A more action-oriented group includes marriage among the institutions needing to be destroyed (O'Neill, 1969; Tomeh, 1975).

A social role is transactional, shaped by the expectations and reactions of those "significant others" among whom the performer plays out his/her life. As women began rewriting the scripts of their "female" role, they necessarily included in their drama the men to whom they were daughters, wives, lovers, colleagues, and so forth. *Unless men stopped classifying women in gender terms, female liberationists would never go beyond a half victory.* (Filene, 1974, p. 234, emphasis added)

The new propaganda stands vigilant over marriages. The clitoris has been isolated and must receive due obeisance in the marriage bed. Love must be made—or sex must be had—a prescribed number of times a week; otherwise one falls from grace and competition. Orgasms must be at least matched in number between the pair, though preferably wife will overtake husband. The Queen of the bed has become reigning monarch, the King her consort. Her grandmother submitted; she will exact the service due according to the marriage contract. Her nature, she has learned, is highly passionate. The male-centered world deprived her of natural outlet throughout all history. She has been made a slave, she has been used in the service of his pleasure with no thought given to her own. Now she moves to conquer. The penis will be hers; it will rise and fall to her imperious command. (Perutz, 1972, p. 97)

Last, but certainly *not* least, consider this quote from Dixon (1969):

The institution of marriage is the chief vehicle for the perpetuation of the oppression of women; it is through the role of wife that the subjugation of women is maintained. . . . Looking at marriage from a detached point of view, one may well ask why anyone gets married, much less women. (p. 57)

Viewing the world from the darkness of this perspective, it is entirely reasonable for Dixon to question whether marriage is a good choice for a woman. With such an attitude, the woman would bring precious little in the way of joy and optimism into the marriage. With special reference to the excerpt from Perutz, a man would be well advised to flee in horror from any woman who would turn the conjugal bed into a combat zone.

Should men marry? That question is one that every man must ask for himself long before he binds himself to the rights and responsibilities of marriage. Some might question whether "bind" is the appropriate word, but I believe it is. A pledge given in a vow is a serious matter: a man demeans himself when he allows the first crisis to undermine his oath to "love and cherish." A few marriages are dysfunctional at the outset, others become so over a period of time. Such a marriage should be terminated, obviously the sooner the better. But one argument, even a series of arguments, is no sign of irreconcilable difference. If the marriage is troubled, counseling can help to determine if issues in the marriage can be resolved. Greer (1971) coined the phrase "symbiosis of mutual dependence," which might be interpreted as lending support to the observation that "the woman is narrowed by the home and the man is narrowed by the woman" (Gilman, 1972, p. 277). Should a man marry? If he is so inclined, he should. On the other hand, he must be vigilant to ensure that he does not become narrowed by the woman. If he does decide to marry, he must (to paraphrase Greer) seek out symbiosis of pleasurable dependence.

## THE THEORY OF MARRIAGE

The emotionally mature male is relatively independent and self-directed. He has mastered the art of self-discipline and maintains a reasonable level of personal control. The typical adult male seeks to enter into a lasting monogamous, heterosexual relationship, and most of his dating from early adolescence onward is part of his preparation. This extended period of time, from early adolescence to adulthood, provides him with the opportunity to meet a variety of girls and women, and in time the individual male will narrow his pursuit to one or several in terms of experience and new-found priorities. But to state this is to state the ideal; the reality may be somewhat different.

One of the most important tasks in late adolescence and early adulthood is successful negotiation of the autoplastic–alloplastic continuum. Both terms are psychoanalytic in origin, but the interactive model of personality makes use of them to describe (1) the impact of the environment on the individual, and (2) the impact of the individual on the environment. The alloplastic individual *acts* upon his *real* environment, and this *act* carries with it the implication of *managing*. In a general sense, the person who is alloplastic controls his environment; the environment shapes the behavior of the person described as autoplastic.

From a psychoanalytic perspective, autoplasty is the earlier phase, in which the individual learns to modify or change his intrapsychic processes in order to *adapt to* his environment. However, in an interactive model of personality, maintaining a high level of personal control means that the individual is *acting* as well as *reacting* in the process of *adapting* to his environment; that is, he needs to be as competent in the one as he is in the other, but the emotionally mature individual will generally manage rather than be managed. Since most role conditioning is as pervasive as it is continuous, the process often does not come to its simple and logical end. The parent(s) and/or significant other(s) may realize that the maturational interests of the adolescent can best be served by encouraging that side of his nature that strives for independence. But these others may not recognize the adolescent's growing need for independence, *or* they may be unable or unwilling to provide the level of support required, and this will spell trouble for all concerned. In most cases, and in one way or another, the adolescent will assert his freedom and independence. If he has to struggle too mightily to attain these, he might come to believe that he must express his freedom through defiance and his independence by alienation.

The defiant, alienated individual—man or woman—is ill-equipped for the stresses and strains of marriage. An important point to grasp is that healthy adjustment emerges from an agreeable and serviceable pattern of behavioral responses, as pleasing for the user as for the significant other. The man or woman who is still reacting, behaving in either a compliant or defiant manner, has not matured in any real sense, and there is a real risk that this person might seek to perpetuate his situation by marrying someone who would serve as either his mentor or foil. According to Dominian (1968), "the survival of every marriage depends on the capacity of the partners to meet the psychological needs which in turn requires a sufficient degree of maturity" (p. 39).

Schoenberg (1981) stated the theory underlying marriage by noting that "marriage is considered a solution for sexual, psychological, and financial needs" (p. 70). However, if these are the needs that encourage the couple to marry, how is it possible that they can be so easily transformed into the usual arguments for divorce? What happens, sometimes in a relatively short period of time, to turn a love into a hate?

### Sexual Needs

In theory, the best sex comes in an intense relationship. Masters and Johnson (1976) argue that it is this sense of commitment, which they refer to as the pleasure bond, that heightens sexual responsivity. Moy (1981) states that "sharing a sexual experience . . . is the most intimate form of communication. When caring, trusting, autonomous verbal communication is used to enhance the total experience, it is bonding for both partners and increases the intimacy in the total relationship" (p. 201). But Albee (1977) has observed that sex is becoming more recreational than procreational; depending on how one defines recreational, this might be a factor helping to explain the significant increase in marriage breakdown.

In 1954, Burgess, Wallin, and Schultz noted that while sexual incompatibility is often said to be the major cause of divorce or the failure of marriages, their review of the literature had not found any convincing evidence to support the allegation. Several decades later, it can be argued that the evidence still is not there. Evidence, or the lack of it notwithstanding, the mythology surrounding the sexual relationship between man and woman, husband and wife, is a latent cause of problems for many couples. In 1974, Koestenbaum wrote that "the [sexual] myth . . . is so dangerous that it has destroyed countless marriages, dismembered families, and disrupted promising and meaningful interpersonal relationships" (p. 4). The situation has not changed: therapists who specialize in marriage counseling are routinely met with complaints emerging out of the man's and woman's sexual nature.

Many therapists would agree that there is too much concern about orgasm, both "having" and "giving." Pressure to achieve orgasm can interfere with the experience of other good feelings (Myers, 1976). It is not unusual for a couple to report that they have to "work" to ensure that the female has her orgasm, and that bringing it about does not come easily. In this context, Slater (1974) observed that preoccupation with achievement turns sex more into work than play. May (1963) cautioned that this simplistic procedure could lead to a mechanistic approach to sexuality, a condition that all authorities in the area of human sexuality would agree gets in the way of pleasurable as well as natural sexual responsivity. Parry (1975) wrote that sexual difficulties are concerned usually with disorders of either the direction or the strength of the sexual drive. Between sexual partners within a marriage, direction describes activity and strength measures interest. A study by Westoff (1974) yielded data which indicated that the frequency of intercourse is highest during the period immediately following a marriage and gradually declines with age.

One is reminded of the conversation two men were having in a downtown bar. The first man said that the reason he got married was so that he could have sex three times a week. "Funny," replied his companion, "that's the reason I got divorced." A colleague once described the sexual activity within his marriage with the comment "It's hard as hell to have good sex when the room around you is on fire." Kaplan (1979) explains, "deep angers deriving from power struggles and other interactional problems that have their genesis in parental transferences towards the spouse, as well as anxieties which have their roots in simple communication failures, may disrupt a couple's sexual relationship" (p. 27).

Other factors influence the strength and direction of the sexual drive. Substance abuse can affect strength as well as direction, as can disease or chronic illness. A man concerned with his sexuality should begin his quest for an answer in the office of his physician. When it is discovered that neither the chemical nor the physiological is causal, psychotherapy becomes the treatment of choice. Most sexual problems are psychological in nature and do respond to therapy, but primary factors must never be overlooked.

## Psychological Needs

Legions of people remain married long past the time when it makes any sense to do so. If pressed, one or the other might concede that remaining in a dysfunctional marriage is less of a problem than undergoing the process of separation that leads to divorce. Exceptions exist, but there remains a strong suspicion that for the most part couples remain married because on one level or another their needs are being met.

Saxton (1968) has written that most marriages fall into either intrinsic or utilitarian categories. While the intrinsic marriage is characterized by intensive interpersonal identification and satisfaction, the utilitarian is conflict-habituated, devitalized, and/or passive-congenial. This suggests to me that the intrinsic is happy bordering on the blissfully ignorant, whereas the utilitarian is functional bordering on the dysfunctional. In the category termed utilitarian it would appear that the partners (1) have become used to arguing with each other; (2) have become so tired of arguing that they simply ignore each other; or (3) have reached the stage where they tolerate one another.

When couples first marry, they do appear to be intimately identified with each other, sometimes to the exclusion of all others. Such exclusionary intimacy seems to characterize the relationship between husband and wife for an extended period of time. How extended? For some, a lifetime; for others, the time is reckoned in months, or years, or decades.

Happily married couples seem to develop a spirit of consensus that serves as a guide in problem resolution. Accordingly, creative problem-solving should be the first objective for the married couple. The ability to settle issues in contention before they escalate into major points for confrontation provides infrastructure for good communication. Schoenberg (1981) has referred to the *blurred-feelings* syndrome in which couples refrain from openness in order to avoid unpleasantness or hurt feelings. It is paradoxical that working to avoid hurt feelings can lead to a breakdown in communication, but it happens. It also happens that one partner will talk excessively, to the extent that the spouse will literally grow tired of listening. Other problems are mislabeled. Case in point: it is not a communication problem when partners fail to listen. Or fail to agree. The more appropriate term for refusing to hear is selective inattention; for differing opinions, independent judgment. Moreover, a spouse should have the right to remain silent. Some people do not want to talk about themselves, and their wishes should be respected. Armchair therapists to the contrary, *not* wanting to talk about personal issues is no vice. If the individual wants to talk about himself, but cannot bring himself to do so, therapy is indicated; but otherwise the person should be left alone.

Sex, on the other hand, is a means of communication: the word "intercourse" provides the clue, and a husband and wife should strive to make their sexual encounters communication at its highest level.

### Financial Needs

The writer remembers listening to an undergraduate professor struggling to explain the difference between the kinds of problems that people have. Two cases were presented, and the students were asked to determine which person faced the more serious problem. In the first case, a woman had written to an advice columnist asking how or where she might find the strength to carry on with her life. The woman reported that her husband was terminally ill, one son was in jail, and the other was an addict. The second case, also a woman, had written that she was severely depressed because financial reverses would require the family to resign from their country club. Each student in the class was required to comment on the two women and their problems. All twenty students in the class agreed that the case of woman number one was far more serious than that of woman number two. However, the professor argued that it was truly not possible for anyone external to the problem to evaluate possible impact. In all cases problems are relative and hinge completely on one's perception and experience, and within that context it is not really possible for any observer to make an absolute determination of their impact or severity.

Thus it is with financial needs within a marriage. For some, getting by is enough; for others, only getting by will simply not do. At one time, husband and wife had to live on the man's salary. In the contemporary marriage, such is not the case. A large number of women, possibly a majority, now work outside the home. The average single salary is not enough to support the couple beyond the basics. It is not difficult to form an impression that most young couples want more than the basics.

A ship with no destination drifts and is carried along by the prevailing tides, now up, now down, groaning and creaking in the high seas, tranquil and lovely in the calm. It does exactly as the sea does. Many marriages are like this. They stay afloat but they have no direction. The priority decision input in their decision making is, what are other people doing? They conform to their social circle in attire, housing, raising children, values, and thinking. "As long as others are doing it, it must be OK," is their standard of what to do. If "everyone" is buying a certain kind of luxury automobile, they also will buy one, even if their time-payment coupon books already constitute a library of monthly bad news. They have not built their own set of independent values concerned with their own particular realities and therefore frequently end up disillusioned and in debt. (Harris, 1967, p. 140)

If a person grows up exposed to certain standards in his home, he is likely going to want to maintain or better them in his own marriage. A traditional view of marriage held that a woman's financial future depended on the earning ability of her husband, and this notion has managed to prevail even though the tradition has passed out of sight. In many marriages the second income seems to be discretional.

Although not typical, there has been a gradual increase in the number of marriages in which the working wife earns more than the husband. The question invariably arises, how does a man accept such a set of circumstances? In general, men do not seem to be too concerned about this unless their situation is very unusual. And even then, the critical factor may not be that of money at all. A number of factors underlie marital adjustment, and the couple's financial condition is rarely of critical import unless other more serious problems have surfaced. The man who is unemployed or working at a minimum wage might come to resent his wife's earnings if they represent a continuing reminder of his inability to provide. Extremely large differences in income might provoke resentment if the man senses that others regard him as being kept. The bottom line is that some men still equate earning power with virility, and may need help in coming to terms with income disparity.

In a general sense, the financial needs of the couple are met when there is income sufficient to permit them to have a life style consistent with their needs and expectations.

## THE REALITY OF MARRIAGE

In addressing the issue of the more liberal view of marriage, Schoenberg (1981) wrote,

One would hope that with this kind of liberation and reduced pressure to initiate marriage, combined with the means to effectively assert one's independence to opt out of an unrewarding marital relationship, there would result better unions. However, what seems to be occurring with great frequency is something quite different: the increase in personal freedom has been accompanied by a *decrease* in personal accountability. Rather than working within the marriage to achieve stability and permanence through compromises and understanding, people are finding it easier to abandon the contract. (p. 78)

But "building a new life of my own" has been until very recently almost exclusively a woman's right: the man has not been as fortunate. In the same chapter, Schoenberg (1981) wrote that by custom and by law, men have been forced to bear financial responsibility for the failed marriage, enabling women to walk away from the marriage without financial cost or risk. Divorce laws per se, and especially those relating to alimony and child support, are anachronistic and greatly in need of change. Fortunately this is happening.

The concepts of marriage are changing, yet the problem attendant on change on any level is basically that of learning the new rules. What seems to be happening is that people—men and women alike—are giving lip-service to change but are continuing to operate as if there had not been any. This divergence can bring about a time warp between theory and reality, which on an individual couple's level is translated on the one hand into how they fantasize their marriage and on the other into disappointment with what is actually happening within their relationship. Marriage is a deep emotional relationship. The husband commits himself to his wife, the wife commits herself to her husband. Couples sometimes make the mistake of believing that togetherness is the essence of faithfulness, smothering each other in the process. The man needs a life of his own independent of his wife, the wife needs a life of her own independent of her husband. Part of the cherished belief system surrounding marriage is that a couple must become a unit exclusionary of all others, which to a certain extent has validity. But only to the certain extent that each finds comfortable. The medical sexologist Lonny Myers (1977), in "A Couple Can Also Be Two People," advocates that the couple take the time to "compartmentalize" their marriage.

Compartment I is the time/energy spent with one's spouse; Compartment II is the time/energy spent on family matters (with or without children) but specifically not with one's spouse. Compartment III is nonfamily time; time/energy given to work, community projects . . . when one is not accompanied by spouse or children, but time that is completely "open" to inspection; one's spouse can know exactly what one is doing and with whom. Compartment IV is time/energy allotted to privacy, time when activities are limited only by one's conscience, sense of responsibility, and ability. (p. 343)

Clinical observations provide strong support for the notion of compartmentalization. Trust is the essential element: it is the kind of trust that says to the partner, "I trust you and know that you will never do anything willingly that will do damage to me or to our relationship."

# References

Albee, G. (1977). The Protestant ethic, sex, and psychotherapy. *American Psychologist*, *32*, 150–61.

Albert, E. M. (1966). The unmothered woman. In S. M. Farber and R. H. Wilson (eds.), *The challenge to women* (pp. 38–49). New York: Basic Books.

Amiel, B. (1984, September). The politics of sexual harassment. *Maclean's*, p. 9.

Andreas, C. (1971). *Sex and caste in America*. Englewood Cliffs, N.J.: Prentice-Hall.

Bednarik, K. (1970). *The male in crisis*. New York: Alfred A. Knopf.

Bem, S. L. (1974). The measurement of psychological androgyny. *Journal of Consulting and Clinical Psychology*, *42*(2), 155–62.

———. (1975). Sex role adaptability: One consequence of psychological androgyny. *Journal of Personality and Social Psychology*, *31*(4), 634–43.

Benson, L. (1968). *Fatherhood: A sociological perspective*. New York: Random House.

Bernard, J. (1975). *Women, wives, mothers: Values and options*. Chicago: Aldine Publishing.

Blair, R. (1981). Homosexuality. In D. Brown (ed.), *Sexuality in America* (pp. 137–42). Ann Arbor, Mich.: Greenfield Books.

Blos, P. (1941). *The adolescent personality*. New York: Appleton-Century-Crofts.

Bowen, E. (1987, May). Ethics: Looking to its roots. *Time*, pp. 28–35.

Brenton, M. (1966). *The American male*. New York: Coward-McCann.

Breuer, J., & Freud, S. (1961). *Studies on hysteria*. Boston: Beacon Press.

Brittan, A. (1989). *Masculinity and power*. New York: Basil Blackwell.

Bryce, J. (1966). The nature of public opinion. In B. Berelson and M. Jenowitz (eds.), *Reader in public opinion and communication* (pp. 13–19). New York: The Free Press.

Burgess, E.; Wallin, P.; & Schultz, G. (1954). *Courtship, engagement and marriage*. Philadelphia: J. B. Lippincott.

Carden, M. L. (1974). *The new feminist movement*. New York: Russell Sage Foundation.

Cayo, P. S. (1969). *The feminized male: Classrooms, white collars and the decline of manliness*. New York: Random House.

Chafetz, J. S. (1974). *Masculine/feminine or human? An overview of the sociology of sex roles.* Irasca, Ill.: F. E. Peacock.

Clark, D. (1974). Homosexuality encounter: In all-male groups. In J. Pleck and J. Sawyer (eds.), *Men and masculinity* (pp. 88–93). Englewood Cliffs, N.J.: Prentice-Hall.

Cochran, L. R. (1978a). Conceptions of man as guides to living. In B. M. Schoenberg (ed.), *A handbook for the college and university counseling center* (pp. 3–23). Westport, Conn.: Greenwood Press.

———. (1978b). Issues in the development of academic support services. In B. M. Schoenberg (ed.), *A handbook for the college and university counseling center* (pp. 203–22). Westport, Conn.: Greenwood Press.

———. (1985). *Position and the nature of personhood: An approach to the understanding of persons.* Westport, Conn.: Greenwood Press.

Cox, S. (ed.). (1976). *Female psychology: The emerging self.* Chicago: Science Research Associates.

de Rougemont, D. (1966). *Love in the Western world.* Greenwich, Conn.: Fawcett Publications.

Dixon, M. (1969, December). The rise of women's liberation. *Ramparts*, 30.

Dominian, J. (1968). *Marital breakdown.* Chicago: Franciscan Herald Press.

Doob, L. (1935). *Propaganda: Its psychology and technique.* New York: Praeger.

Duberman, L. (1975). *Gender and sex in society.* New York: Praeger.

Eisenstein, Z. R. (1981). *The radical future of liberal feminism.* New York: Longman.

Ellul, J. (1968). *Propaganda: The formation of men's attitudes.* New York: Alfred A. Knopf.

English, H. B., & English, A. C. (1958). *A comprehensive dictionary of psychological and psychoanalytical terms: A guide to usage.* New York: David McKay Company.

Erikson, E. H. (1959). *Identity and the life cycle.* New York: International Universities Press.

Evans, E., & Potter, T. (1970). Identity crisis: A brief perspective. In E. D. Evans (ed.), *Adolescents: Readings in behavior and development* (pp. 53–68). Hinsdale, Ill.: Dryden Press.

Farrell, W. T. (1975). Beyond masculinity: Liberating men and their relationships with women. In L. Duberman, *Gender and sex in society* (pp. 216–47). New York: Praeger.

Fasteau, M. (1974). *The male machine.* New York: McGraw-Hill.

Festinger, L. (1957). *A theory of cognitive dissonance.* Stanford, Calif.: Stanford University Press.

Filene, P. (1974). *Him/her/self: Sex roles in modern America.* New York: Harcourt, Brace, Jovanovich.

Frankl, V. (1966). Self transcendence as a human phenomenon. *Journal of Humanistic Psychology*, 6(2), 97–106.

Frankl, V. E. (1977). *Man's search for meaning.* New York: Pocket Books.

Freeman, J. (1976). The social construction of the second sex. In S. Cox (ed.), *Female psychology: The emerging self* (pp. 136–51). Chicago: Science Research Associates.

Fried, M. H. (1969). Mankind excluding woman [Review of *Men in Groups*]. *Science*, 165, 883–84.

Friedenberg, E. (1959). *The vanishing adolescent.* Boston: Beacon Press.

Fromm, E. (1956). *The art of loving.* New York: Harper & Row.

————. (1972). *Escape from freedom*. New York: Avon Books.

Fullerton, G. P. (1977). *Survival in marriage: Introduction to family interaction, conflicts, and alternative*. Hinsdale, Ill.: Dryden Press.

Gadpaille, W. J. (1972). Research into the physiology of maleness and femaleness. *Archives of General Psychiatry, 26,* 193–206.

Garai, J. E., & Scheinfeld, A. (1968). Sex differences in mental and behavioral traits. *Genetic Psychology Monograph, 77,* 169–299.

Gilman, C. (1972). *The home: Its work and influence*. Urbana, Ill.: University of Illinois Press.

Goldberg, H. (1976). *The hazards of being male*. New York: Nash Publishing.

Goldberg, S. (1973). *The inevitability of patriarchy*. New York: William Morrow and Company.

Goldenson, R. M. (1970). *The encyclopedia of human behavior: Psychology, psychiatry and mental health*. Garden City, N.Y.: Doubleday and Company.

Gordon, B., and Meth, R. (1990). Men as husbands. In R. Meth and R. Pasick (eds.), *Men in therapy*. New York: Guilford.

Graham, M., & Stark-Adamec, C. (1978). The complexity of attitudes toward women: I. Personal attitudes and their sources. *International Journal of Women's Studies, 1*(5), 482–502.

Green, M. (1976). *Fathering*. New York: McGraw Hill.

Greer, G. (1971). *The female eunuch*. New York: McGraw-Hill.

Guze, S. (1992). *Why psychiatry is a branch of medicine*. New York/Oxford: Oxford University Press.

Haggarty, J. (1975). *Sex in prison*. New York: Ace Books.

Harris, T. A. (1967). *I'm ok—you're ok*. New York: Harper & Row.

Hilgard, E. R. (1962). *Introduction of psychology*. New York: Harcourt, Brace and World.

Hitler, A. (1971). *Mein Kampf*. (trans. R. Mainheim). Boston: Houghton-Mifflin.

Horrocks, J. (1969). *The psychology of adolescence*. Boston: Houghton-Mifflin.

Hutt, C. (1972). *Males and females*. Harmondsworth, England: Penguin Books.

Hutt, M.; Isaacson, R.; & Blum, M. (1966). *Psychology: The science of interpersonal behavior*. London: Harper & Row.

Jersild, A. (1960). *Child psychology*. Englewood Cliffs, N.J.: Prentice-Hall.

Johnson, W. (1986). *The future is not what it used to be*. New York: Dodd, Mead & Company.

Kaplan, H. S. (1979). *Disorders of sexual desire*. New York: Brunner/Mazel.

Kaplan, L. (1965). *Foundations of human behavior*. New York: Harper & Row.

Katz, D. (1966). The functional approach to the study of attitudes. In B. Berelson and M. Janowitz, *Reader in Public Opinion and Communication* (pp. 51–64). New York: The Free Press.

Kaufman, S. A. (1981). *Sexual sabotage: How to enjoy sex in spite of physical and emotional problems*. New York: Macmillan.

Kelly, G. A. (1955). *The psychology of personal constructs*. New York: W. W. Norton.

Kendler, H. H. (1963). *Basic psychology*. New York: Appleton-Century-Crofts.

Kessler, S. J., & McKenna, W. (1978). *Gender: An ethnomethodological approach*. New York: John Wiley and Sons.

Kinsey, A.; Pomeroy, W.; & Martin, C. (1948). *Sexual behavior in the human male*. Philadelphia: W. B. Saunders.

Koestenbaum, P. (1974). *Existential sexuality: Choosing to love*. Englewood Cliffs, N.J.: Prentice-Hall.

Komarovsky, M. (1976). *Dilemmas of masculinity: A study of college youth*. New York: W. W. Norton.

Lazarus, R., & Folkman, S. (1984). Coping and adaptation. In W. Gentry (ed.), *Handbook of behavioral medicine* (pp. 282–325). New York: The Guilford Press.

Lederer, W., & Jackson, D. (1968). *The mirages of marriage*. New York: W. W. Norton.

Levinson, D.; Darrow, C.; Klein, E.; Levinson, M.; & McKee, B. (1978). *The seasons of a man's life*. New York: Alfred A. Knopf.

Lewin, K. (1935). *A dynamic theory of personality*. New York: McGraw-Hill.

Lidz, T. (1968). *The person: His development through the life cycle*. New York: Basic Books.

Luft, J. (1970). *Group processes: An introduction to group dynamics*. Palo Alto, Calif.: Mayfield Publishing Company.

Lynn, D. B. (1964). Divergent feedback and sex-role identification in boys and men. *Merrill-Palmer Quarterly, 10*, 17–23.

Maslow, A. (1954). *Motivation and personality*. New York: Harper & Row.

Maslow, A. H. (1955). Deficiency motivation and growth motivation. In M. R. Jones (ed.), *Nebraska symposium on motivation* (pp. 1–30). Lincoln: University of Nebraska Press.

Masters, W. H., & Johnson, V. E. (1974). *The pleasure bond: A new look at sexuality and commitment*. Boston: Little, Brown & Company.

———. (1976). *The pleasure bond*. New York: Bantam.

May, R. (1963). What is our problem? *Review of Existential Psychology and Psychiatry, 3*(2), 109–12.

McCary, J. (1973). *Human sexuality*. New York: Van Nostrand.

Mead, M. (1967). *Male and female*. New York: William Morrow.

Millett, K. (1970). *Sexual politics*. Garden City, N.J.: Doubleday & Company.

Money, J., & Ehrhardt, A. A. (1972). *Man and woman: Boy and girl*. Baltimore, Md.: Johns Hopkins University Press.

Money, J.; Hampson, J. G.; & Hampson, J. L. (1955). An examination of some basic sexual concepts: The evidence of human hermaphroditism. *Bulletin of the Johns Hopkins Hospital, 97*, 301–19.

Mount, E., Jr. (1973). *The feminine factor*. Richmond, Va.: John Knox Press.

Moy, C. (1981). Communicating sexuality. In D. Brown (ed.), *Sexuality in America* (pp. 185–202). Ann Arbor, Mich.: Greenfield Books.

Murphy, G. (1960). *Human potentialities*. London: George Allen and Unwin.

Mussen, P., & Rutherford, E. (1963). Parent-child relations and parental personality in relation to young children's sex role preference. *Child Development, 34*, 589–607.

Myers, L. (1976). Orgasm: An evaluation. In S. Gordon & R. Libby (eds.), *Sexuality today and tomorrow* (pp. 281–86). Scituate, Mass.: Duxbury Press.

———. (1977). A couple can also be two people. In R. Libby & R. Whitehurst (eds.), *Marriage and alternatives: Exploring intimate relationships* (pp. 335–46). Glenview, Ill.: Scott Foresman.

O'Neill, W. (1969). *Everyone was brave: The rise and fall of feminism in America*. Chicago: Quadrangle Press.

Page, S. (1987). On gender roles and perception of maladjustment. *Canadian Psychology, 28*(1), 53–59.

Parry, R. (1975). *A guide to counselling and basic psychotherapy.* Edinburgh: Churchill Livingstone.

Perutz, K. (1972). *Marriage is hell.* New York: William Morrow.

Pindell, R. (1983). Verbicide: The perilously leaning tower of babble. *English Journal, 72*(5), 50.

Pyke, S. W., & Stark-Adamec, C. (1981). Canadian feminism and psychology: The first decade. *Canadian Psychology, 22*(1), 38–54.

Rogers, C. R. (1951). *Client-centered therapy.* Cambridge, Mass.: The Riverside Press.

Rosen, H. (1977). *Pathway to Piaget.* Cherry Hill, N.J.: Postgraduate International, Inc.

Rossi, A. S. (1964). Equality between the sexes: An immodest proposal. In R. J. Lifton (ed.), *The Woman in America* (pp. 98–143). Boston: Houghton-Mifflin.

Roszak, B., & Roszak, T. (eds.). (1969). *Masculine/feminine: Readings in sexual mythology and the liberation of women.* New York: Harper & Row.

Sandler, J.; Myerson, M.; & Kinder, B. N. (1980). *Human sexuality: Current perspectives.* Tampa, Fla.: Mariner Publishing Company.

Sargent, A. (1977). *Beyond sex roles.* St. Paul, Minn.: West Publishing Company.

Saxton, L. (1968). *The individual, marriage, and the family.* Belmont, Calif.: Wadsworth Publishing Company.

Schiller, P. (1981). *The sex profession.* Washington, D.C.: Chilmark House.

Schoenberg, B. M. (1975). *A strange breed of cat: An encounter in human sexuality.* Palm Springs, Calif.: ETC Publications.

———. (1981). Marriage. In D. Brown (ed.), *Sexuality in America* (pp. 69–84). Ann Arbor, Mich.: Greenfield Books.

Schoenberg, B. M., & Preston, C. F. (eds.). (1983). *Interactive counseling.* Westport, Conn.: Greenwood Press.

Schoeppe, A.; Haggard, E.; & Havighurst, R. (1953). Some factors affecting sixteen-year-olds' success in five developmental tasks. *Journal of Abnormal and Social Psychology, 48,* 42–52.

Scott, J. (1958). *Aggression.* Chicago: University of Chicago Press.

Seidler, V. J. (1989). *Rediscovering masculinity.* New York: Routledge.

Sexton, P. (1969). *The feminized male.* New York: Random House.

Silverman, H. (1981). Female sexuality: Singlehood and the problems of intimacy. In D. Brown (ed.), *Sexuality in America* (pp. 43–67). Ann Arbor, Mich.: Greenfield Books.

Slater, P. (1974). *Earthwalk.* Garden City, N.J.: Doubleday & Company.

Smith, H. C. (1968). *Personality development.* New York: McGraw-Hill.

Stansby, C. (ed.). (1972). *Strip Jack naked.* London: Gentry Books.

Steinem, G. (1972). The myth of masculine mystique. *Journal of International Education, 1*(2), 30–35.

Stoll, C. S. (ed.). (1973). *Sexism: Scientific debates.* Reading, Mass.: Addison-Wesley.

Strang, R. (1957). *The adolescent views himself.* New York: McGraw-Hill.

Takacs, M. (1983). Man power. *Quest, 12*(4), 71.

Toffler, A. (1971). *Future shock.* New York: Random House.

Tollison, C. D., & Adams, H. E. (1979). *Sexual disorders: Treatment, theory, research.* New York: Gardner Press.

Tolson, A. (1977). *The limits to masculinity.* London: Tavistock Publications.

Tomeh, A. (1975). *The family and sex roles.* Toronto: Holt, Rinehart and Winston of Canada.

Vance, B. (1990). Loving without limits. In F. Abbott (ed.), *Men and intimacy*. Freedom, Calif.: The Crossing Press.

Vilar, E. (1972). *The manipulated man*. New York: Farrar, Straus and Giroux.

Weisstein, N. (1976). Psychology constructs the female. In S. Cox (ed.), *Female psychology: The emerging self* (pp. 91–103). Chicago: Science Research Associates.

Weitz, S. (1977). *Sex roles: Biological, psychological and social foundations*. New York: Oxford University Press.

Wesley, F., & Wesley, C. (1977). *Sex role psychology*. New York: Human Sciences Press.

Westermarck, E. (1936). *The future of marriage in western civilization*. New York: Macmillan.

Westoff, C. (1974). Coital frequency and contraception. *Family Planning Perspectives*, *6*(3), 136–41.

Wideman, R., & Clarke, J. (1987, January). Understanding self-image: A guide for educators. *Guidance and Counselling*, 2(3), 24–31.

Winokur, D. (1973). Does anybody really need psychotherapy? Consequences for retaining a mental illness mode. *Psychotherapy, Theory, Research and Practice*, *10*(1), 41–43.

# Index

## About the Author

B. MARK SCHOENBERG is Director of University Counselling Centre, Memorial University of Newfoundland, and is a psychologist in private practice. He is the author of *A Handbook and Guide to the College and University Counselling Center* (1978) and *Bereavement Counselling: A Multi-disciplinary Handbook* (Greenwood, 1980).